DATA NINJA

A Game Plan For Success in Data Analytics

Game Plan
Your 5-Point Game Plan For Success

✓ **Master Excel**

✓ **Conquer SQL and RDBMS**

✓ **Tame Data Integration and Warehousing**

✓ **Pickup Coding**

✓ **Continue Adapting**

Every effort has been made in the preparation of this book to ensure the accuracy of the information presented. However, the information contained in this book is sold without warranty, either express or implied. Neither the author, nor the publishing company, nor its dealer and distributors will be held liable for any damages caused or alleged to be caused directly or indirectly by this book.

First Edition

Edited by Zander Tsadwa

Printed in the United States of America

DATA NINJA

A Game Plan For Success in Data Analytics

> **Data are becoming the new raw material of business.**
> ~ Craig Mundie

www.frulouis.com

> A man who uses an imaginary map thinking that it is a true one, is likely to be worse off than someone with no map at all.

~ Ernst Schumacher

Dedication

Writing a book is a release and a burden. For one, it's a hard, time-consuming journey to get it done. On the other hand, the author gets to work with and be helped by a vast network of people to see it through.

Anyone who knows me well knows me to be a talker. Rarely am I lost for words. But here I am. The appreciation and gratitude I feel for people in my life that influenced and guided me into making this book possible are beyond words.

First, I dedicate this book to my parents, Martin and Esther, for without them bringing me into this world and their unconditional love, I wouldn't be here writing a book. You define what it means to be great every day. Your wisdom and trust are my fuel.

To my uncle and second father, Joseph Fru, I'm infinitely grateful. He saw the spark early in me and never stopped pushing, mentoring, and supporting me all the way. I'm forever grateful for your exuberance and your example.

To my siblings, your unconditional love and support have always been the bedrock of my being. Thank you.

To my mentors and content creators from all over the world, gracias, danke, miyaka, merci beaucoup! I could fill this entire book with names, but you know who you are. Bosses, peers, friends, teachers, authors, content creators—thank you. I wasn't born with knowledge in my head. Everything I know today was taught to me by someone out there. The books I've read, the links I've referenced, the commentaries I've shared, and much more are all thanks to you. Plain and simple, a reference book like this would not be possible without you all.

I want to give thanks to my students, mentees, and the countless number of people I've been blessed to cross paths with. Young people, recent college graduates, immigrants, or anyone looking to better their lives and realize their dreams—thank you. This book is yours. You are the source of inspiration for this book, and I hope you get out of it as much as I have received from writing it.

Last, but certainly not least, thanks to Zander Tsadwa for the editing, writing assistance, patience, counsel, guidance, and support to see it through. The original drafts of this book are nothing like the pages you're going through today.

Table of Contents

Introduction

Exciting Times

"We're entering a new world in which data may be more important than software."
~Tim O'Reilly, Founder, O'Reilly Media

We live in arguably the most exciting time in history. The spread of technological innovation is changing the way we live our lives and do business. This is all precipitated by the insurmountable amount of data users generate and companies have at their disposal to gain insights and influence their bottom lines. This is a revolution happening right before our very eyes that will touch every business, industry, and life on this planet. The numbers (pun intended) don't lie, and here are a few to blow your mind:

- The amount of information man created from the dawn of civilization until 2003 is currently created every two days! (Bernard Marr)
- 5 quintillion bytes of data are generated by internet users on a daily basis (Bernard Marr)
- Data is growing faster than ever before and by the year 2020, about 7 megabytes of new information will be created every second for every human being on the planet (Bernard Marr)
- A 10% increase in the data accessibility for Fortune 1000 companies is likely to increase their income by $65 million! (Bernard Marr)

These numbers are staggering, to say the least. Yet, out of all the data we create, only about 5% of it (Bernard Marr), is analyzed and put to use. This means there is a huge amount of data that remains untapped. Just imagine the potential here. Silicon Valley giants like Google, Amazon, Microsoft, and Facebook are already taking advantage of this to build massive businesses with great success. Even better, more and more "regular" companies on the sidelines are seeing the value data can have on their businesses and are clamoring to get in on the frenzy.

As a result, a lucrative field is emerging and companies have great need to employ data professionals—*Data Ninjas*—who can come in and make sense of it all. You can become a part of this wave. This book will inspire you, offer a game plan, and give you the resources to learn and to start working with data.

Meet Patrick

"The future belongs to those who believe in the beauty of their dreams."
~Eleanor Roosevelt

I had no intention of writing this book until the events of a cold January morning in 2017 inspired me to do so. It was a Thursday morning and I was up a little early. The day started normally as I made my way through traffic and icy roads straight to the gym for a quick workout. Exhausted from my cardio routine, I looked forward to the comfort of my daily pre-work shower. I was expecting a call or a text from my student Patrick about a job he recently interviewed for, but it did not come yet. He was supposed to text me by 7:30 a.m. How did it go? What could have gone wrong? Did he get the job? This and many more questions flew through my mind. Showering became unimportant as I sat there contemplating.

I was mired in a cycle of excitement and worry about Patrick's future for about fifteen minutes. By this time, the smell of sweat was whistling at me to hop in the shower. As I stretched my arm to grab the phone, it then vibrated. The timing was perfect. I hesitated and then went for it. Two taps on the screen later and I was quickly greeted with a text from Patrick—he got the job.

TODAY

Man fru I can't thank you enough for your help. I was offered a job at the state yesterday. I interviewed with them Thursday. Really really appreciate your support

9:21 AM

A text from Patrick to Fru after landing a job

Patrick had approached me a few months ago about getting into technology and working with Big Data. And for the months leading up to that text, I coached him, offered tutorials in my basement, met with him over the phone, and whatever else it took to get Patrick up to speed with key tech concepts. We formed a **game plan**. We mapped out what he knew, what he didn't know, and how he was going to bridge the gaps. Patrick stuck to the game plan and became a learning machine. He gobbled up all the links and resources I shared with him and even found some I was unfamiliar with in his daily studies. We both learned. The intense studying and knowledge exchange soon became routine.

Patrick had gotten several interviews for IT positions but didn't get any offers. He didn't lose hope though. After every rejection, he identified weak points in his skills and knowledge and made it a priority to learn even more. All of that studying, coaching, interviewing, rejection, and more studying led to the moment of me covered in dried sweat reading his celebratory text. His life was changed that day. It reminds me of *The Pursuit of Happyness* starring Will Smith. Patrick worked hard, never gave up, and eventually achieved his goals.

Patrick's story is not an exception. There are many professionals like Patrick: people who do not like their current jobs, people who want to earn more, people who want to do something more fulfilling. Many people like the career prospects of data analytics, but don't know where to start. They can learn a lot, but virtually all aspiring data analytics professionals hesitate when faced with the daunting question, "*What* should I learn?"

Some Perspective

"When you change the way you look at things, the things you look at change."

After Patrick and I worked and word of his success spread locally, the number of people who approached me for guidance on getting into the data analytics field grew. These are mostly immigrants, students, or entry-level professionals with varying levels of technological background.

Some of them come from doing Warehouse jobs picking and packing freight. Some are recent college graduates who need a roadmap and some hand-holding as they enter the real world. Some are professionals who, for one reason or another, have fallen behind and are looking for ways to level up in the digital age. Others might have seen something in the news, heard me talk, or have been convinced by a friend or loved one that the Data revolution coming and they want to be a part of it.

Regardless of the impetus, the aspirations are the same. People are curious and need help. And I dare say, experts in the field aren't doing a good enough job nurturing, guiding, and showing the ropes to the new ones, so we're missing out on a huge talent pool—especially immigrants, minorities, and people without strong technical backgrounds. Without guidance on what to learn, people get frustrated and give up! It's sad to see as they not only give up on their dreams of working in technology, they give up on their dreams of a better life entirely.

I can relate with the frustration as I myself am a living example. I've always been the curious, techy, geeky type, but my background and education throughout high school was royally inadequate for the demands of the Western world. I remember in one of my high school computer classes (circa 2004), the teacher came to class and asked us to draw a computer and name the parts for our warm-up exercise. Yes, I mean draw, there were no actual computers to work on. So, we had to draw the mouse, keyboard, monitor, and CPU tower. Imagine coming home with your grade book to your parents with an "A" in computer science, but all you did was draw. One has to wonder if that made us better artists or technologists. Go figure!

Again, I'm not sharing this to shoot down on any educational system or teaching approach. People have to make do with their resources and circumstances. That simply was the circumstance of my time and we made do with it. I'm sharing this to draw some perspective. Without perspective, we miss the ability to relate to one another. But in today's world, reality demands much more from us. Whether you're an immigrant or not, the challenges of your background alone won't give you a job. Empathy for your story won't replace answers to the technical questions you'd be asked during a job interview. Too many people are on the sidelines looking in. We need to get past the fluff and offer tactical and practical advice to people. Learning and positioning yourself for success within the system is what people need, and that's what this book offers.

With the people I've encountered looking to get into technology and data analytics, the biggest issue isn't that they're incompetent or can't learn the concepts. Far from it. Oftentimes, they simply don't know what they don't know. That's the dagger, the poison, the killer of dreams. My goal is to eradicate that with a **game plan**.

No battle was ever won according to plan, but no battle was ever won without one.
~Dwight D. Eisenhower

A game plan takes out the guesswork. It's a tried and tested strategy. That's why top athletes and elite sports teams, militaries, corporations, and nations all have game plans. Any endeavor worth undertaking shouldn't be done without one.

If you're worried that you aren't advanced enough to make use of this book, don't be. No experience required! This book is a simple, valuable game plan for entry-level IT workers with no technical background looking to work in the field of data analytics. In fact, anyone regardless of age, sex, race, or technical experience can get tremendous value out of the game plan and resources presented.

Scaling Patrick's Story

Find out what you like doing best, and get someone to pay you for doing it.
~Katharine Whitehorn

Many moons before I started writing this book, I organized a number of free events in an effort to evangelize and spread this idea of a game plan to aspiring data analytics professionals. At those events, I spoke about what people with absolutely no skill or experience in IT need to learn. I brought in some of my friends and colleagues who are experts and have been in the field for years to share their experiences and offer advice. I even invited some of my contacts who were recruiters and staffing agents to join in. Afterall, once people mastered the concepts, they'd need jobs.

Free Events Organized by Fru on getting into Data Analytics (2017)

These events were great and hugely successful. But, as I quickly realized, it was a double-edged sword. Good in the sense of giving exposure to my message and offering a game plan to more people, and bad in that with more exposure came more demand. So, this book is my attempt at scaling those free events by offering the **game plan** in a book. Anyone, anywhere, whether on a bus, a plane, in a coffee shop, or the comfort of their own home can employ these tips and resources to get into and be successful in the booming field of data analytics.

Is This You?

Have you heard the buzz around data today, but don't know what it's all about, or what's in it for you? Here are some questions to consider:

- Do you constantly check your bank account every day, wishing you had a career that paid a little more?
- Are you currently eyeing some new analytics-related career opportunities, but are afraid to make the leap?
- Is your current job getting bothersome because analytics is coming and you are not properly trained for some of the new tools and demands?
- Have you been curious to learn about things like Excel, SQL, Data warehousing, but have no links or resources to start with?

If you answered "Yes," to any of the questions above, then this book surely is for you. The 5-Point Game Plan for Success in Data Analytics takes you below the surface, demystifies the fears, and introduces you to the world of data professionals.

If you are serious about working with Data, it's not enough to just talk about it. You have to actually do it. You need to cultivate and nurture your Data Ninja skills; become stealthy, efficient, and ready for anything.

Packed full of tips, tricks, and numerous free resources, this book is a must-read for anyone working with data in today's market, newbies and veterans alike.

Are you ready to become a Data Ninja?

What I Bring To The Table

"Some things cannot be taught; they must be experienced. You never learn the most valuable lessons in life until you go through your own journey."
~ Roy T. Bennett

Over the last few years, I've been at the forefront of the Data Wave as a practicing Data Ninja. Data Ninja is a term I use to describe anyone who works with data since it requires so many skills and tools. I wear many hats and have worked in a wide variety of roles ranging from, Data Warehousing Expert, Solutions Architect, Big Data, Pre-Sales Engineer, and most recently Machine Learning, AI, and other emerging technologies. I even run a LinkedIn group called **Enterprise Data Analytics Ninjas**.

In my various roles and engagements, I do webinars, roadshows, have discussions with directors, VPs, and top C-level executives about their data strategies, and have spoken at countless data-related events, meetups, and conferences. With such a wide exposure to the industry, my perspective goes beyond theory into practice. My hand is constantly on the pulse as I speak with and interact with hundreds if not thousands of companies looking to revamp their data and analytics architecture to better respond to the ever-changing and increasingly complex reality we face. I see and hear first-hand what companies are *actually* doing and what they need from a skillset perspective. And that's what I'm presenting.

Naturally, I have an architect's mindset and prefer to see the big picture first, hence the roadmap or game plan. Once you have your game plan, the details can be sorted out easily.

As I worked with Patrick and many others students, I collected my thoughts, perspectives, experiences, and resources into little articles and notes. The **5-Point Game Plan for Success in Data Analytics** is a result of that, and the resources included are the exact same resources I've used to study and elevate my competency. That said, this game plan is not a bible. Remain open to new information and changing realities, but use this book as a starting point.

What This Book Is About

This book will inspire you by presenting a solid game plan for success. Beyond inspiration though, the book is meant to be 100% tactical. You will be exposed to many concepts, along with a rich library of resources in each chapter to help you learn the concepts in depth. In the end, you'll be presented with compelling stories of individuals like Patrick who've changed their lives and are making a difference in the companies they work for because they had a game plan that they executed well.

At the end of the day, I wouldn't have done my job if you finished without having a game plan for yourself or a useful place to start. Whether you take it sequentially as presented here, or some variation of it, be sure to have a game plan. It's that important.

"Start with the end in mind. "
~ Stephen R. Covey

If you doubt your game plan, talk to somebody. Ask for help. Seek a mentor or coach to guide you further along the way. You've got to spend as much effort formulating your game plan as you do actually learning the tools and concepts of data analytics.

I once heard someone say that if he were given five minutes to chop down the biggest tree in all of the Northwest or else die, he would spend three of those five minutes sharpening his ax. I think that the lesson applies here. *Sharpen your ax* so that your cut is more effective as you start your journey into the field of data analytics.

This is the book I wish I had read when I started on my own data analytics journey helping companies get value out of their data assets. So, grab a coffee and get focused. Let's get started on turning you into a Data Ninja.

What This Book Is NOT About

This is not a book to teach you about a particular technology or sell you on a certain vendor. I want to emphasize this early on as technology professionals notoriously fall into camps and are very territorial about which tools they use. If you're just getting started in the field, don't let the motley mixtures of vendors and tools distract you. Focus on the essential concepts, and the rest will fall into place.

Take ETL for example, a concept discussed in this book. There are many tools in the market that can do ETL (extract, transform, load). But the concept of ETL itself doesn't change across the tools. What does it mean to extract, transform and load data? Why do companies do it in the first place? How do companies do it? What are the steps or processes involved? These are the things you've got to master first, the underlying concepts. Once you understand the fundamental concepts well, you can always zero-in to master tools from specific vendors as the need arises (e.g. learning and getting certified in a particular ETL tool like Talend, SSIS, or Informatica).

But, I must caution. Don't get caught up in the vicious cycle of developing a myopic view too early and being a tool fanatic. Being a good data professional is about using technology to solve business problems. As a beginner, you've got to focus on the *ends*, regardless of which tool you use.

This book will expose you to a broad set of concepts and offer resources. You will be inspired to go out and learn. The sacrosanct process of learning is ultimately about exposure to variety, not indoctrination in the ways of some specific tool, vendor, or company.

PART ONE

Whetting the Appetite

The Exponential Growth Of Data

A book about data analytics wouldn't be complete without first acknowledging the exponential growth in data we are experiencing. The world today is awash with data, and the far-reaching tentacles of data touch nearly all aspects of our lives. Data influences everything from how we communicate with loved ones to how we bank our money and get access to health care.

Companies of all shapes and sizes are experiencing the effects of this data boom. Projections of about 40% compounding growth year to year into the next decade are not uncommon to see.

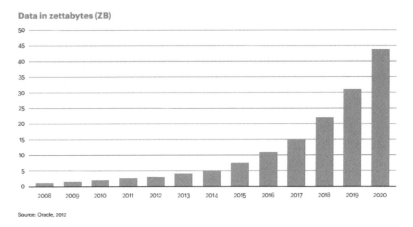

Figure 6, data growth outlook. (Oracle)

Dazzling facts about the current growth of data

- It is expected that by 2020 the amount of digital information in existence will have grown from 3.2 zettabytes today to 40 zettabytes.
- The total amount of data being captured and stored by industries

doubles every 1.2 years.

- Every minute, we send 204 million emails, generate 1.8 million Facebook likes, send 278 thousand Tweets, and upload 200,000 photos to Facebook.
- Google alone processes on average over 40 thousand search queries per second, making it over 3.5 billion in a single day.
- Around 100 hours of video are uploaded to YouTube every minute and it would take you around 15 years to watch every video uploaded by users in one day.
- 570 new websites spring into existence every minute of every day.
- Today's data centers occupy an area of land equal in size to almost 6,000 football fields.
- The NSA is thought to analyze 1.6% of all global internet traffic—around 30 petabytes (30 million gigabytes) every day.
- The number of bits of information stored in the digital universe is thought to have exceeded the number of stars in the physical universe in 2007.
- Retailers could increase their profit margins by more than 60% through the full exploitation of big data analytics.

(Marr)

Some More Data Analytics Facts and Data Trends

- Business analytics is a $12.2 billion industry, according to Gartner Inc.
- McKinsey & Company forecasted a shortage by 2018 of professionals specializing in the data analytics field.
- Every dollar that a company invests in business analytics earns $10.66, according to Nucleus Research.
- According to Forrester Research, 97% of companies with revenue of more than $100 million are pursuing expertise in business analytics.

(Kristal)

Numbers don't lie! With more than 2 quintillion bytes of new data being generated every single day, we now see companies, corporate managers, and executives scramble to hire individuals who understand data and can work with it to derive competitive value. For the Data Ninjas out there, this should be music to your ears as this burgeoning demand from businesses not only translates to immediate job openings, but also long-term job security and strong take home salaries.

The Sexiest Job

Before we get into the nuts and bolts of the Data Ninja game plan, let's take a look at the hiring outlook for Data Professionals.

As the amount of web and digital data steadily grows, most reputable research firms in the industry are predicting a significant upsurge in the hiring of data analytics professionals. Because of the extremely high demands, some have even gone as far as calling professionals who work with data—Data Ninjas— the *sexiest job of the 21st century.*

Hiring Numbers

According to a report published by McKinsey & Company's Business Technology Office in 2011 entitled *Big data: The next frontier for innovation, competition, and productivity,* data has swept into every industry and business function and is now an important factor of production, alongside labor and capital. This observation underscores the great opportunities that lie ahead for businesses and the need for strong Data Ninja-type talent to get into the game.

> "The United States alone faces a shortage of 140,000 to 190,000 people with deep analytical skills as well as 1.5 million managers and analysts to analyze big data and make decisions based on their findings."

(McKinsey)

Research firm Gartner cited many industries and companies as having a great need for people skilled in managing and analyzing data:

> "By 2015, big data demand will reach 4.4 million jobs globally, but only one-third of those jobs will be filled. The demand for big data is growing, and enterprises will need to reassess their competencies and skills to respond to this opportunity. Jobs that are filled will result in real financial and competitive benefits for organizations. An important aspect of the challenge in filling these jobs lies in the fact that enterprises need people with new skills—data management, analytics and business expertise and nontraditional skills necessary for extracting the value of big data, as well as artists and designers for data visualization."

(Gartner)

Even though the statistics and articles presented by some research firms explicitly make references to "Big Data" (a topic more advanced than the intended scope of this book), I nonetheless see the move to Big Data analytics as a natural career progression for any person working in the data field.

Back in a 2009 press release, IBM expressed interest in the need to open a global network of Advanced Analytics Centers. The expectation was to use these worldwide centers to retrain or hire up to 4,000 additional data professionals.

> "ARMONK, N.Y. - 28 Apr 2009: IBM(NYSE: IBM) today announced a significant expansion of its capabilities around business analytics with plans to open a network of Analytics Solution Centers around the world, beginning with five in the second quarter of 2009. These initial centers will be located in Tokyo, London, New York City, Beijing and Washington, D.C. As part of this initiative, IBM will retrain or hire as many as 4,000 new analytics consultants and professionals."
>
> (IBM)

An article by Allison Stadd goes further to illustrate the need and demand for data professionals.

> It's not just the skills needed, it's also the raw manpower. In a survey by Robert Half Technology of 1,400 U.S.-based CIOs, 53% of the respondents whose companies are actively gathering data said they lacked sufficient staff to access that data and extract insights from it. Translation: you are sorely needed.
>
> (Stadd)

In addition to the hiring demand and shortage of labor expressed above, we also see the job postings for data professionals remaining steadily high.

A search done on job site Glassdoor.com resulted in over 102,305 job positions being listed with **Data Analyst** tags.

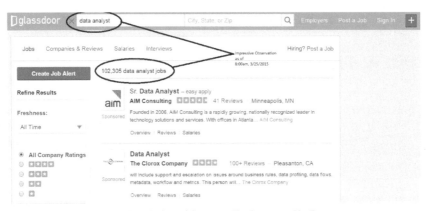

Figure 2, Data Analysts job listings on GlassDoor.com. (GlassDoor)

A similar search done on tech-oriented career site Dice.com came up with equally impressive numbers for data analytics-related job openings. More than 40,000 jobs were listed in their database.

Figure 3, Data Analyst job search of Dice.com (Dice)

These numbers all indicate a very strong outlook in the jobs market for data professionals and underscore the point that data is the way of the future. There is a great need for skilled professionals who aspire to make a career out of working with data and you can be a part of that wave.

How Much do Data Ninjas Make?

Not everyone getting into the field of data analytics cares about the money or salary ranges. But to be honest, most do. It's the primary motivation, and rightly so. Bills need to be paid and life needs to be lived. Because of this, salary considerations are important for both aspiring or practicing Data Ninjas. Here, we'd explore some of the numbers, salaries, and incentives that come with the job.

A quick internet search will undoubtedly present a wide-ranging pay spectrum for data professionals. According to the talent firm **DataJobs,** national salary ranges for a few data-related job titles are as follows:

Job Title	Level of Expertise	Pay Range
Data Analyst	Entry Level	$50,000-$75,000
Data Analyst	Experienced	$65,000-$110,000
Data Scientist	N/A	$85,000-$170,000
Database Administrator	Entry Level	$50,000-$70,000
Database Administrator	Experienced	$70,000-$120,000
Data Engineer	Junior	$70,000-$115,000
Data Engineer	Domain Expert	$100,000-$165,000

Figure 4, pay range of data professionals. (Big Data Salary) - https://datajobs.com/big-data-salary

To further substantiate these pay and income numbers, we look at technology consulting firm Robert Half Technology's (RHT) 2015 publication of salary ranges in the chart below:

Job Title	2014	2015	% Change
Big Data Engineer	$110,250 - $152,750	$119,250 - $168,250	9.3%
Database Manager	$107,750 - $149,000	$112,250 - $160,250	6.1%
Database Developer	$ 92,000 - $134,500	$ 98,000 - $144,750	7.2%
Database Administrator	$ 87,500 - $126,000	$ 91,000 - $134,750	5.7%
Data Analyst/Report Writer	$ 67,750 - $101,000	$ 70,750 - $108,250	6.1%
Data Architect	$111,750 - $153,750	$119,750 - $164,750	7.2%
Data Modeler	$ 97,250 - $134,250	$101,750 - $145,250	6.7%
Data Warehouse Manager	$115,250 - $154,250	$119,750 - $163,000	4.9%
Data Warehouse Analyst	$ 99,000 - $133,750	$102,500 - $142,500	5.3%
Business Intelligence Analyst	$101,250 - $142,250	$108,500 - $153,000	7.4%
Electronic Data Interchange (EDI) Specialist	$ 72,250 - $102,250	$ 74,750 - $108,250	4.9%
Portal Administrator	$ 91,250 - $121,000	$ 92,750 - $127,250	3.7%

Figure 5, the salary range for data professionals. (Robert Half Technology)

If numbers are your thing, then these numbers should definitely get you off the chair. No one can guarantee salaries, but we must admit that these salary figures look extremely promising and should give you an idea of what to expect. Especially given that according to the U.S. Census Bureau, the U.S. real (inflation-adjusted) median household income was $51,939 in 2013, and hasn't risen much for the years after that. This means salary for data-related roles are on average significantly higher than the median income numbers reported by the U.S. Census Bureau. As one looks into the future, these numbers can only get better as more data is generated, collected, and stored every single day. Companies are clamoring for talent to come in and help them make sense of it all. And you can be a part of that wave.

Sample: Real World Data Ninja Story

> One of my first real, non-restaurant jobs was as a "Data Analyst" for a really large insurance/healthcare corporation. I worked in the area that managed the marketing database for the company.

For example, we could only market to certain zip codes (by law) and once I had to input something like 10,000 zip codes into a database in about three days.

We would also do a lot of analysis on what groups were more responsive to our marketing campaigns. So I'd end up throwing a ton of information into a spreadsheet (Lotus 123 at the time) and then doing lots of analysis to find the best performing groups (people between the ages of 55-65 who live in non-urban areas of Florida as an example).

Using this info, we'd go out and try to find more people (our target audience) who mirrored the most responsive groups. Purchasing a mailing list or advertisement in certain publications whose readers are similar to these people, like AARP, would be a way in which to target them.

You might be responsible for coming up with the stats for the target audience and then going out and finding them. You'll also spend vast amounts of time in front of a computer inputting and looking at data. You may also work with programmers who may be in India or somewhere else.

In order to do a good job, you'll need to be very detail oriented. You will need to like to work with numbers. Logical/critical thinking skills

Sample : Real World Data Ninja Job Description and Posting

In this section, we present a sample Data Ninja job description. This sample is available free on the resources.workable.com website. I have gone through the job description to highlight the specific skills and requirements that could be of importance to an aspiring Data Ninja.

As mentioned earlier, different companies and industries may have specific job requirements tailored to the specific Data Analytics role that they are looking to fill.

One of the best ways to see the skills and concepts that companies *really want* is to go out and read the postings on job boards. Job postings are a gold mine of information.

Actual Data Analyst Job Posting

Job Title: Data Analyst (WFM) - Contract
Requisition ID 45383 - Posted 03/12/2015 - Temp - COO - Analytics - Austin (Parmer Lane) - Texas - United States - Americas

The Challenge Ahead:
Electronic Arts WW Customer Experience organization is seeking a Contract Data Analyst role to provide Work Force Management (WFM) analytics to support Work Force Management team.

What a Contract Data Analyst does at EA:
Proven record of using analytics to provide actionable insights to drive decision making within the Workforce Management and contact center environments. We are looking for a seasoned analytics Ninja, who takes the data and turns data into insights, insights into stories, stories into actionable recommendations to improve the efficiencies of the contact centers. So, do bring success examples during the interview.
Manage and deliver analytics using different data sources from various different systems.
The role will be doing both the run-the-business analysis and long term analysis for the workforce management team. The role will need to conduct large amount of adhoc, time sensitive analysis work for the stakeholders in a short notice and quick turn-around environment. The role will also do some longer term analysis into chronic WFM issues.
Present results to business leaders, WFM stakeholders and other analysts.
Communicate analytics data throughout the organization in a clear, concise and actionable way.
Work in a highly collaborative team environment both within the group and across business units/functions.

The next great Contract Data Analyst needs:
Ability to deliver analysis in a fast, accurate and timely manner in a very agile and ad hoc environment is a must.
Ability to perform under pressure and make suggestions with imperfect data is a must.
1-3 years of hands-on workforce management experience is a must. Contact center analytics experience is highly preferred. Forecasting experience is highly preferred.
Bachelor's degree is preferred. Background in finance, marketing, economics, computer science, math or other quantitative discipline is preferred.
Expert status in analyzing large, complex, multi-dimensional data sets with a variety of tools.
Understand data warehousing structure (e.g. roles of ETL, BI, facts, dimensions, drill-down, roll-up, data mining)
Expert in SQL is a must
Experience with BI (Tableau, Microstrategy, Crystal Reports, etc.) is highly preferred
Advanced Excel skills is preferred (such as pivot tables, vlookups and arrays)
Knowledge of best practices for data-driven customer experience.
Self-starter with a passion to "tell story with data" and strong attention to the details.
Excellent verbal and written communication skills and the ability to interact professionally with others. Comfortable with presenting data to the leaders at all levels
Experience in the game industry preferred.

Who are you:
Creative: Ability to find out-of-the-box/non-traditional ways of problem solving, and apply innovative thinking when approaching and defining solutions.
Entrepreneurial: Self-directed/motivated individual with the willingness and ability to personally jump in, roll up their sleeves and get to work in either a strategic or executional capacity when needed.
Pro-active: Provides recommendations & takes the lead on initiatives without being prompted by internal or external partners.
Efficient: Highly resourceful and organized person that evaluates everything & implements new ways of doing things faster, better.
Curious/Inquisitive: Investigates the current situation, asks the relevant questions needed to get the whole picture then provides specific actionable recommendations
Team Player: Leader that encourages team collaboration, works well with peers across multiple functionalities within the company, promotes enthusiasm, leverages powers of influence when necessary and motivates relationship building.
High-energy, assertive and decisive person that has strong interpersonal skills and can build rapport and trust quickly in order to form strong business partnerships within the organization as well as outside the company.
Gets it done – Believes that actions speak louder than words, thrives on achievement.

Data analyst job description

Job brief
We are looking for a passionate Data Analyst to turn data into information, information into insight and insight into business decisions.
You will conduct full lifecycle activities to include requirements analysis and design, develop analysis and reporting capabilities, and continuously monitor performance and quality control plans to identify improvements.

Responsibilities
Interpret data, analyze results using statistical techniques and provide ongoing reports
Develop and implement data collection systems and other strategies that optimize statistical efficiency and data quality
Acquire data from primary or secondary data sources and maintain databases/data systems
Identify, analyze, and interpret trends or patterns in complex data sets
Filter and "clean" data, and review computer reports, printouts, and performance indicators to locate and correct code problems
Work closely with management to prioritize business and information needs
Locate and define new process improvement opportunities

Requirements
Proven working experience as a data analyst
Technical expertise regarding data models, database design development, data mining and segmentation techniques
Strong knowledge of and experience with reporting packages (Business Objects etc), databases (SQL etc), programming (XML, Javascript, or ETL frameworks)
Knowledge of statistics and experience using statistical packages for analysing large datasets (Excel, SPSS, SAS etc)
Strong analytical skills with the ability to collect, organise, analyse, and disseminate significant amounts of information with attention to detail and accuracy
Adept at queries, report writing and presenting findings
BS in Mathematics, Economics, Computer Science, Information Management or Statistics

Figure 12, Data Analyst Job Posting. (Workable)

What's In It For You?

Someone looking at the job responsibilities and salivating over the lucrative pay numbers might rightly ask, *What does this all mean for my pocketbook?* Or better still, *What's in it for me?* These are both good questions to ask, and the answer is remarkably simple.

With the growth of data picking up exponentially, increased demand for data professionals, the limited supply of qualified candidates, and salaries increasing year after year, it is clear that aspiring or practicing Data Ninjas all around the world have favorable career outlooks in terms of wage and job prospects for years to come.

Whether your goal is to keep the paychecks coming at a steady rate or you are just looking to advance your career, the field of data analytics is proving to be the place where you can confidently make that happen.

Now that your appetite is whetted, let's get started on the game plan—turning you into a formidable Data Ninja.

Part two

The Game Plan

Master Spreadsheets

> When in doubt,
> Pivot!

Motivation

Welcome to spreadsheets. Some readers at this page will be shocked at seeing a book written about data analytics starting with spreadsheets as the number one tool in the game plan. Rightly so. Spreadsheets (Excel in particular) can be extremely polarizing, with diehards on either side of the fence. But ultimately, engaging in the debate of whether Excel is good or bad for data analytics is futile. As you read, realize my goal in this chapter isn't to convince you to like Excel. Neither am I trying to make the case for why your organization should switch to using spreadsheets for data analytics. Far from it. Spreadsheets are a powerful, versatile, and ubiquitous tool that is found in some shape or form within most organization. As a Data Ninja, it behooves you to be familiar with spreadsheets, or risk missing out on a vital, albeit contentious, data analytics tool.

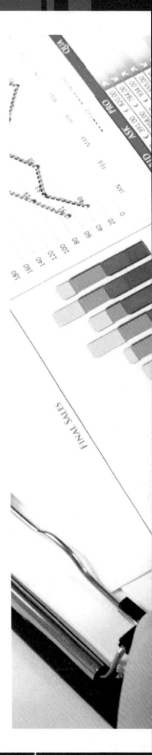

Spreadsheets

There are many spreadsheet-type products in the market: Microsoft Excel, Google Sheets, Zoho Sheets, Smartsheet, Gnumeric, Kspread, LibreOffice Calc, and much more. Some of these products are free, others are not. Some are desktop-based, while others are online-based. Some come with a suite of other products like Word, Powerpoint, Email, and others come as standalone products. But regardless of their unique differences, what these spreadsheet-type products all have in common is they allow users to perform easy calculations, graphing, tabulation, and pivoting of data.

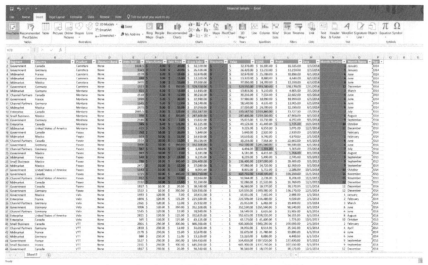

Figure 1: Sample Excel File. Data stored in Rows and Columns

Microsoft Excel is the application with the most market dominance and adoption in its class. For that reason, we'll be using "Excel" and "spreadsheets" interchangeably throughout this chapter, much like "Xerox" can mean "printer" or, "Google it" means "Search it" in everyday parlance.

May Excel Be With You

Excel is a very powerful yet user-friendly tool which has a firm place in the market as far as data manipulation and analytics is concerned. A poll from kdnuggets.com shows Excel in the top-5 of most popular analytical tools being used in the industry today.

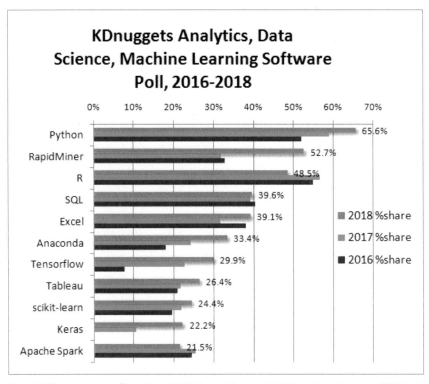

Figure 2, KDnuggets Analytics/Data Science 2018 Software Poll: top tools in 2018, and their share in the 2016-7 polls (Nuggets)

These polling numbers don't lie. Regardless of people telling you how bad Excel is, realize that it's still being used *heavily* within organizations. The ubiquity and versatility of the product gives users the ability to quickly **manipulate, cleanse**, and **merge** data sets with relative ease. That is why it makes it to the top of our list as a product to learn in the data ninja game plan.

MS Excel Core Functionalities

Now that you've been convinced as to why you absolutely should learn MS Excel, we'll go on to identify what exactly about the product you should be learning.

MS Excel offers a rich library of functionalities that are useful for quickly analyzing and working with data. Trying to learn it all in one pass would be a daunting task. I've worked with Excel for years and there are still things about the product I don't know. That said, start with the basics. Then expand as your skills grow, or as your data analytics needs get more sophisticated. Here are the main functionalities to start and gain familiarity with:

Sort: The ability to arrange data in the respective rows and columns in either ascending or descending order.

Filter: The ability to make data results fit a certain criterion and appear a certain way.

Conditional Formatting: Highlighting a specific column or row or a block with any color depending on the value of that block.

Charts: Graphic displays of data results (i.e. charts, graphs) that depict the particular rise or fall in the values (e.g. a profit rise). Graphs represent data better than long lists of numerical values.

Pivot Tables: One of the most powerful Excel tools; allows the user to extract the significance from a detailed data set.

Tables: Properly arranged tables allow one to analyze data in a much faster way.

What-If Analysis: It allows one to try different values in cells in order to see whether the changes will affect the outcome of the formula.

Analysis ToolPak: An Excel add-in program that can perform financial, statistical, and engineering data analysis.

MS Excel For Data Analysis

Data Ribbon

As a Data Ninja, in addition to the aforementioned capabilities, you might find the **data ribbon** in Excel to be one of the most useful of all. This ribbon holds functions that can help anyone quickly perform a variety of statistical and non-statistical calculations on their data. Be sure to get extra familiarity with that ribbon and be able to take advantage of it.

Microsoft Excel Data Ribbon. (Excel)

Data Analysis ToolPak

In addition to the out-of-the-box functions present in the data ribbon, Excel also makes available the Data Analysis ToolPak[1] for use in advanced data analytics scenarios.

The Data Analysis ToolPak (DAT) is especially relevant to you as a Data Ninja because it takes you beyond the everyday additions and summations in Excel. DAT provides a powerful set of tools used for statistical analysis and can help analysts figure out the variance, correlation and covariance of data as well as other features. If you find yourself needing to do these kinds of analyses, then you definitely need to install and master the DAT.

---

[1] The Analysis ToolPak is an add-in that comes with Microsoft Excel.

> If you need to develop complex statistical or engineering analyses, you can save steps and time by using the Analysis ToolPak. You provide the data and parameters for each analysis, and the tool uses the appropriate statistical or engineering macro functions to calculate and display the results in an output table. Some tools generate charts in addition to output tables.
>
> (Office)

MS Excel: Available Data Sources

Before working with data in Excel, you've got to get access to data and bring it to your spreadsheets or workbooks. Luckily, Excel offers a wide variety of ways to access and import data. Below is a list of a few data sources supported by Excel. Be sure to gain familiarity accessing data from these sources:

Example data sources for Analytics in Excel

- From files: Excel, CSV, XML, Text or Folder that contains files.
- From databases: SQL Server, Access, Oracle, IBM DB2, MySQL, PostgreSQL and Teradata.
- From other data sources: SharePoint List, OData feed, Windows Azure Marketplace, Hadoop Distributed File System (HDFS), Windows Azure Blob storage, Windows Azure Table storage, Active Directory, and Facebook.

MS Excel: Data Pivoting

As a Data Ninja, you may be required to spend a lot of time summarizing data because people prefer looking at summaries. Pivoting is an incredibly powerful and easy way to tabulate and summarize data. Though there are many products in the market with pivoting functionality, Excel's ubiquity makes its pivot table one of the most widely used.

The good thing about the pivot functionality in Excel (or any other pivot tool for that matter) is that it allows analysts to quickly change how data is summarized with very little effort.

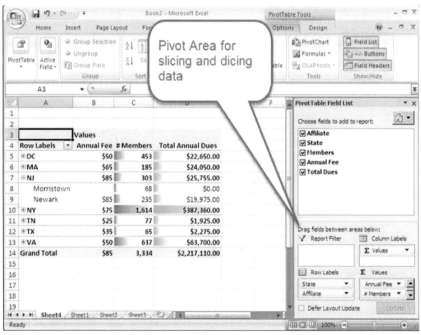

Figure 2, Microsoft Excel screenshot. (Excel)

Whether you want to summarize daily sales data for your company by line of business (LOB), or sum employees' total working hours for the week, pivot tables will let you do that with relative ease. As a Data Ninja, mastering pivot tables is an important skill to have in the game plan.

MS Excel: Data Presentation And Visualization

Another extremely important feature within excel is that of presentation. As a Data Ninja, your job isn't over after you've performed your analysis or created pivot tables. The results from any data analysis work done usually don't stay in a vacuum. High level executives who typically consume data or the fruits of your labor need it to be presented in clean and intuitive visualizations. Once again, lucky you! Microsoft Excel stands out in this aspect, offering a ton of outside-the-box display and visualization capabilities.

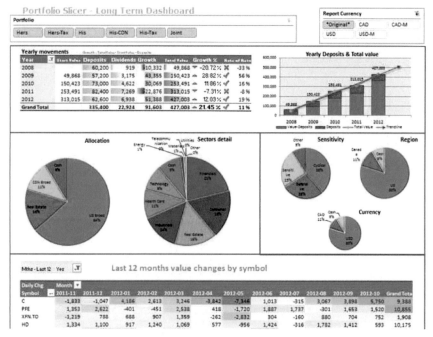

Figure 4, the sky's the limit for using Microsoft Excel for dashboarding and presentation of data that tells a colorful and coherent story. (Excel)

Here are some of the common presentation and visualization functions within Excel you should be familiar with:

- Pie Charts
- Maps
- KPIs (Key Performance Indicators)
- Hierarchies
- Drill Up and Drill Down
- Background Color and Background Images
- Hyperlinks

Microsoft PowerBI

In recent years, Microsoft has been working to develop a number of integrated components for data collection, analysis, and visualization. The goal is to offer a one-stop shop for enterprise level data analytics within organization. The name has changed over the years, but the current iteration of these products are being distributed under the name *Power BI*.

As a Data Analytics Ninja, Power BI is something you should be familiar with. The "BI" stands for Business Intelligence. Power BI is not one single tool, but a collection of tools that form an ecosystem. Some of the products within the Power BI ecosystem include the following:

Power Pivot

Power Pivot provides end-user accessible in-memory data modeling for large data sets. Power Pivot was introduced as an add-in to Excel 2010, and has since been fully integrated as an out-of-the-box feature in Excel 2013.

Power View

Power View is a complimentary technology to Power Pivot, enabling advanced visualizations for data models created in Power Pivot. Power View delivers interactive visualizations, including animated visuals and maps powered by Bing Maps. Originally, Power View was available only as a SharePoint feature. It has since been integrated directly into Excel 2013.

Power Map

Power Map, previously known by the development name GeoFlow, is an add-in to Excel 2013 that provides more compelling Bing Map-powered visualizations, extending Power View's capabilities with 3D map visualizations.

Power Query

Power Query, previously known by the development name Data Explorer, is an add-in to Excel 2013 that provides a more fluid, open data discovery environment than is provided by Power Pivot alone.

In Microsoft We Trust

Love it or hate it, Microsoft is everywhere. By leveraging the popularity and versatility of spreadsheets, Microsoft has worked on providing users with rich capabilities for quickly accessing, analyzing, and presenting data. The good thing is you don't have to be an expert to do this. That's why Excel is so popular.

And with the emergence of Power BI, even more people are getting empowered to work with data. It is truly exciting to say the least, and will potentially redefine the way data analysis is done within organizations. That's why as a Data Ninja, you certainly can't ignore the suite of solutions Microsoft offers—or do so at your own peril.

> PowerBI seems to hold a lot of promise and because of this Microsoft is laying a great stake in it.
>
> **Microsoft** is not content to let Excel define the company's reputation among the world's data analysts. That's the message the company sent on Tuesday when it announced that its Power BI product is now free. According to a company executive, the move could expand Microsoft's reach in the business intelligence space by 10 times.
>
> If you're familiar with **Power BI**, you might understand why Microsoft is pitching this as such a big deal. It's a self-service data analysis tool that's **based on natural language queries** and advanced visualization options. It already offers live connections to a handful of popular cloud services, such as **Salesforce.com, Marketo** and GitHub. It is delivered as a cloud service, although there's a downloadable tool that lets users work with data on their laptops and publish the reports to a cloud dashboard.

(Gigaom)

What Excel Is Not

Ok. Now that we've spent a great deal of time hyping up Excel and talking how great it is, permit me to throw some cold water on your fire before you go find a tattoo artist to ink "MS Excel" on your forehead.

MS Excel is a very versatile tool that plays a pivotal role in the data analysis process for most companies. But MS Excel doesn't come without its drawbacks. As such, it's essential to have an understanding of what MS Excel *is* and *is not*.

> "Let's face it: We all have seen a crazy Microsoft Excel spreadsheet or encountered one of its dreaded "Not Responding" messages. Unfortunately, the flexibility and ease of Excel makes it the ideal candidate for inappropriate use and widespread abuse.
>
> Modern Excel 2013 and the latest Power BI add-ins do sizzle in demonstrations, but there are analyses that simply do not make sense to use Excel for today.
>
> (Datanami)

Here are some pain points you might encounter working with MS Excel.

Pain Points With MS Ecxel

Collaboration: MS Excel is inherently designed for personal use and for single-user access at a time. Spreadsheets tend to be shared via email, which causes duplicate copies or inconsistent data.

Maintenance: With data coming from different sources, it can be difficult to maintain spreadsheets manually, especially if the data changes frequently.

Data Integrity: With multiple users having the capability to make copies of any spreadsheet with ease, it becomes difficult to control who or where the single version of truth lies potentially causing serious data integrity issues.

Accessibility: Being a desktop-based application, on-the-go access is not possible except when you have a compatible mobile gadget such as a laptop.

Data Security: Excel data is usually downloaded and made locally available to user machines. This makes the spreadsheets not only error-prone, but also susceptible to theft and data loss.

Scalability: There are times when spreadsheets get so big that it doesn't make any sense to hold the data in Excel. The new Power Pivot side of Excel compresses and handles more data than traditional Excel alone. However, capacity will still be constrained to the user's CPU and storage since all the processing is done on the local desktop or laptop.

I hope this assessment of MS Excel's strengths and flaws has given you a good idea of why it should be in your Data Ninja game plan. If you've been putting Excel aside, don't. Take time to learn it and get comfortable with it.

Not a Panacea

As mentioned earlier, the point of this book is not to debate whether MS Excel or Power BI is good or bad as an analytical tool, but rather to appreciate that they both have strong potentials and are backed by a formidable company in the technology space. MS Excel offers a lot of functionalities, but does not solve all problems faced by companies today and should not be seen as the panacea. No single tool is, for that matter.

Throughout my career, I've seen companies willing to go to the far reaches of the solar system in order to prevent people from using Excel or spreadsheets as their enterprise analytical tool. But despite all the effort, most users default to opening up Excel when they encounter any data set that needs quick formulas and calculations.

Trying to stamp out Excel as an analytical tool is akin to preventing employees from accessing the company's WiFi. Sure, you can do it. Yes, there are legitimate grounds for doing it. But should you? What are you giving up when you do that? The same questions apply to negative attitudes toward Excel. The ubiquity and nimbleness of the tool makes it a force to be reckoned with. As a Data Ninja, you've got to master it and have it in your game plan.

I'm fully aware also that learning Spreadsheets sounds trivial. That, being proficient in Excel might not seem exciting or interesting as some of the other tools out there. But believe me, it's like knowing how to parallel park a car. No one applauds you for knowing how to do it. You can go years without needing to do it. But when the moment comes, and you've got four passengers in your car, all looking at you to do the job, that's not the time to make excuses, argue why parking is not necessary, or why cars are bad for the planet. Your incompetence will show. Just learn how to park the damn car before you ever need it. In the same vein, just learn how to use spreadsheets (MS Excel) before you need it. Thank me later.

Ninja Tip

Choosing between Excel and some other solutions for your data analytics purposes is not an either/or proposition, nor is it a zero-sum game.

Excel has capabilities that are proven to be very valuable for certain types of data analysis. The point of this book is to encourage you as a Data Ninja to go out, explore the tool further, and use it when you see fit.

Summary

In this game plan, we have presented a good suite of concepts and features that Excel provides which can help companies and their analysts do wonders with data. I have also tried to present some of the drawbacks that can come with building enterprise-wide solutions on spreadsheet tools like MS Excel. It's only fair that we get both sides of the picture.

Below, I've compiled a list of some of the best and most relevant resources for learning Excel. The tool itself is like an onion. I don't expect you on your Data Ninja journey to master every single functionality it offers. Be selective. Get started with what you need, and as you encounter more situations or analytical needs, you can dive deeper to peel back more layers of the onion. Beyond the resources provided, when in doubt, consult Google or YouTube.

Long gone are the days of relying solely on binders or large print books that promptly get outdated as soon as a new version of a product is released. Today, the internet and search engines can give you the most up-to-date tips and tricks on any tool you want to master—Excel included.

So, in addition to the links and resources I've provided you in this game plan, I would encourage you to go further and search. You'll be pleasantly surprised by the wealth of information available for you to get started building your Excel ninja skills.

Resources Center

About the icons used below:

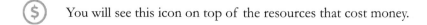 You will see this icon on top of the resources that cost money.

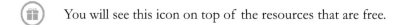 You will see this icon on top of the resources that are free.

GCF Learn Free

GCF Learn Free will teach you how to create formulas. They will guide you through the basics of creating formulas for any kind of spreadsheet. They also give you opportunities to practice with real-world scenarios.

http://www.gcflearnfree.org/excelformulas

Chandoo

Chandoo has a straightforward approach to learning Excel. They cover the basics and gradually move you along into advanced knowledge. They go over everything from formulas and charts to VBA, dashboards, and more.

http://chandoo.org/wp/

Five Minute Lessons

Just like the name suggests, this site offers five minute lessons to bring you to the next level in Excel. These are short lessons but teach important skills that everyone should know in Excel.

http://fiveminutelessons.com/learn-microsoft-excel

Excel Exposure

Excel totes the Microsoft Most Valuable Professional badge on their landing page. They have tons of resources and video tutorials that can take you from beginner to advanced user. Their lessons include videos, infographics, and workbooks.
http://excelexposure.com/

Trump Excel

"An effort to learn and share amazing tricks on Excel spreadsheets." Trump Excel focuses more on tips and tricks rather than walking through the basics. Trump Excel assumes the user already has a basic knowledge but wants to learn some new things. Even if you are a beginner, you will pick up some interesting tricks here that you might not find on your own.
http://trumpexcel.com/

Excel Tip of The Month

Excel expert Isaac Gottlieb created this site to give monthly tips. This is another straightforward site that focuses on tips and tricks rather than guiding you through from start to finish. This site will continue to give you useful tips even when you've become comfortable working in Excel.
http://isaacgottlieb.com/tip-of-the-month

Excel Tips

You guessed it, more tips and tricks. Excel is a program that is so immersive you will probably never fully master it. That isn't meant to discourage you, but rather encourage you to learn everything you can.
http://excelribbon.tips.net/

Peltier

Peltier is a blog that focuses on Excel charts. They have pages on pages of Excel charts and how-to guides. If you are struggling with charts in Excel, this is the place for you.
http://peltiertech.com/

Excel Central

Excel Central offers videos, eBooks, and file downloads. They sell courses and books, but they will let you view the first eight chapters in their courses for free to see if it is right for you. Not a very fancy website, but they do have some good essential information here.
http://excelcentral.com/

How Cast

How Cast provides short-form instructional video and text content. They do not specifically concentrate on Excel, but their videos are a great way to get started.
http://www.howcast.com/guides/573-How-to-Use-Microsoft-Excel/

PC World: "Use Microsoft Excel for Everything"

This is an excellent article about Excel that enlighten you on its many uses.
http://www.pcworld.com/article/229504/five_excel_nightmares_and_how_to_fix_them.html

Lynda

> There is just no escaping Lynda's vast categories of tutorials. Lynda is a paid service that offers a huge list of different kinds of tutorials and videos, a great resource for anyone who wishes to expand their knowledge on pretty much any subject.
> http://www.lynda.com/search?q=excel

 # Key NINJA Lessons

✓ Don't let the simplicity fool you. Excel is a powerful tool that can do wonders in augmenting your Data Ninja skills.

✓ In addition to learning Excel and the basics, strive to take it a step further.

- Learn to extend Excel using add-ins and scale using SharePoint and Office 365.
- Learn PowerBI — including Power Pivot, Power Query, Power View, Power Maps — and other "Power" products that extends the capabilities of native Excel.

✓ Excel is here and will be around for a while. So, ignore anyone telling you otherwise and just learn it. As a Data Ninja you've got to be comfortable with the basic concepts discussed in this chapter.

✓ Being proficient in Excel might not seem exotic, but it's an important stepping stone in your journey to becoming a well-rounded and unstoppable Data Analytics Ninja.

2

Conquer
SQL and RDBMS

 "A man walks into a bar and sees two tables. Says 'Can I join you?'"

Motivation

Now things will get a bit more complex. In the world of data analytics, this means needing more *structure*.

Before we dive into the intricacies of this particular chapter, let's take a step back and let our imaginations go to work. Can you think of a time when someone told you a story or explained something to you, and by the end of it you were completely lost? Even more confused than when you began? Maybe you read a book (hopefully not this one), and at the end you found yourself begging for more information. Or maybe you watched a movie and had no idea what was going on. I'm not judging anyone in particular, just stating that confusion often results from a lack of *structure*. Whether it's someone explaining a concept to you, a book you read, or a movie you watched, it is extremely hard to make sense of something if it lacks structure.

Computer scientists know that having structure to data is essential to performing analytics. So, they came up with a language for giving structure to data and hence understanding data. This chapter will talk about that language, Structured Query Language (SQL), and why it's an absolutely essential tool to have in your toolbelt as a Data Ninja.

What Is SQL?

Structured Query language (SQL)—pronounced as *sequel* or *ess-queue-ell*—is the primary language used to request information from a database, and it is used *everywhere*.

For example, a database-driven dynamic web page takes user input from forms and clicks, then uses it to compose a SQL query that retrieves information from the database required to generate the next web page.

Even more astounding is the fact that all Android phones and iPhones have easy access to a SQL database called SQLite and many applications on your phone use it directly.

Today, many of the applications that run our banks, hospitals, universities, governments, and small businesses eventually touch something running SQL.

The ubiquity makes SQL an incredibly powerful tool and it has proven itself over the years to be a very successful and solid technology worth mastering.

Why Is SQL Beneficial

SQL is especially beneficial because it provides some standardization to the way data in databases can be queried. It is tremendously flexible, powerful, and very accessible, which makes it simple to master. Some of the key benefits of using SQL to store and manage data over spreadsheets are listed below:

1. You can query and make updates to data in databases.
2. You can look up data from a database very quickly.
3. You can relate data from two different tables together using JOINs.
4. You can create meaningful reports from data in a database.
5. Your data has a built-in structure to it.

6. Information of a given type is always stored only once.
7. SQL Databases can handle very large data sets (compared to Excel spreadsheets).
8. SQL Databases are concurrent—multiple users can use them at the same time without corrupting the data.
9. SQL Databases scale well beyond the data volumes of what can be handled in Excel spreadsheets.

With SQL, you can build databases, enter data into the databases, manipulate data, and query the database data with relative ease. That is why SQL rises to the top of skills to master as part of the Data Ninja game plan.

Data Analysis With SQL

SQL statements are divided into two main categories: DML (Data Modification Language) and DDL (Data Definition Language). Below, we provide a high-level overview of these two categories of SQL and their common features.

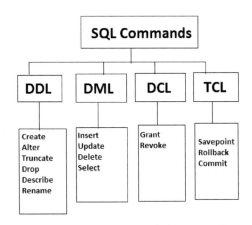

Figure 5: Which programming tools to use for data analysis (kdnuggets)

Data Definition Language (DDL)

DDL statements are used to build and modify the structure of objects in a database. These database objects include views, schemas, tables, indexes, etc. Some examples of DDL statements:

Example SQL DDL:

- CREATE - create objects in the database.
- ALTER - alter the structure of the database.
- DROP - delete objects from the database.
- TRUNCATE - remove all records from a table.
- RENAME - rename an object.

Data Manipulation Language (DML)

DMLs manipulate data. As such, they are usually used for inserting data into database tables, retrieving existing data, deleting data from existing tables and modifying existing data. DML touches only data and never modifies the schema of the database (table features, relationships, and so on).

Example SQL DML:

- SELECT
- UPDATE and INSERT statements
- JOINS
- DISTINCT
- IN
- BETWEEN
- LIKE
- GROUP BY
- ORDER BY
- PARTITION BY
- AGGREGATE FUNCTIONS such as AVG, MIN, MAX, SUM, COUNT, etc.

The processes performed by DML statements are what a Data Ninja may be tasked with performing on a day-to-day basis. That is why it is recommended for all aspiring data ninjas to be proficient or at least familiar with the concepts of writing SQL DML statements.

Data Control Language (DCL) and Others

In addition to DMLs and DDLs, there are more advanced topics in SQL used for interacting with the RDBMS. DCL (Data Control Language) and TCL (Transaction Control Language) are used to manage transaction integrity, security around the data, and more.

Data Control Language (DCL) is used to create roles, permissions, and referential integrity as well as to control access to a database by securing it.

Example SQL DCL:

- GRANT - give users access privileges to database
- REVOKE - withdraw access privileges given with the GRANT command
- EXECUTE AS – run as

Transaction Control (TCL) statements are used to manage the changes made by DML statements. They allow statements to be grouped together into logical transactions.

Example SQL TCL

- COMMIT - save work done.
- SAVEPOINT - identify a point in a transaction to which you can later roll back.
- ROLLBACK - restore database to original since the last COMMIT.
- SET TRANSACTION - Change transaction options such as isolation level and which rollback segment to use.

RDBMS Systems

At the core of SQL is the Relational Database Management System (RDBMS). An RDBMS is a program that lets you create, update, and administer a relational database. In an RDBMS, data is structured in database tables, fields, and records. Tables within the RDBMS might be related by common fields for easy cross-table querying.

There are many vendors supplying RDBMS products in the market—some of which are proprietary and some which are open-sourced. A few examples of these RDBMS systems include: PostgreSQL, SQLite, MySQL, MSSQL Server, Oracle, Teradata, Netezza, and Sybase.

Key Characteristics Of The RDBMS

1. Data is stored in a set of tables. Each RDBMS table consists of database table rows. Each database table row consists of one or more database table fields.
2. Rows represent records, and columns represent record attributes or fields.
3. Each row in the table is usually identified by a primary key that uniquely identifies the record to other systems.
4. Every row in the same table has exactly the same number of columns (even though some of the column values might be NULL)
5. RDBMS uses data manipulation language (SQL) for querying and manipulating data in the RBDMS.
6. RDBMS uses several design patterns to reduce duplication of data in database (Normalization).
7. ACID is a concept utilized to keep transactions reliable. The acronym refers to the four key properties of a transaction: Atomicity, Consistency, Isolation, and Durability.
   - **Atomicity:** All changes to data are performed as if they are a single operation.
   - **Consistency:** Data is in the same state when a transaction starts and when it ends.
   - **Isolation:** The intermediate state of a transaction is invisible to other transactions.
   - **Durability:** After a transaction successfully completes, changes to data persist and are not undone, even in the event of a system failure.

Database Administrators

Enterprise RDBMS systems such as Microsoft's SQL Server, Oracle DB, MySQL and IBM's DB2 are complex applications that call for specialized knowledge and training. As a result, some organizations hire dedicated database administrators (DBA) to manage and administrate their RDBMS environments.

The role of Database Administrator (DBA), is charged with the creation, maintenance, backups, querying, tuning, user rights assignment, and security of an organization's databases. Some tasks include:

- Installation, configuration and upgrading of RDBMS software and related products
- Establishing and maintaining sound backup and recovery policies and procedures
- Taking care of the database design and implementation
- Implementing and maintaining database security (i.e. create and maintain users and roles, assign privileges)
- Database tuning and performance monitoring
- Application tuning and performance monitoring
- Setup and maintenance of documentation and standards
- Planning growth and changes (capacity planning)
- General technical troubleshooting and consultation to development teams

DBA is a popular and lucrative field in itself and warrants an entire game plan book of its own. As a Data Ninja, you might find yourself interacting with DBAs or playing the DBA role entirely for some smaller organizations. So, understanding the role and functions of a DBA is vital in your journey to becoming a skilled Data Ninja.

Summary

- A lot of the data in existence today is stored in RDBMS databases and SQL is the premier interface used to access and manipulate this data.

- Your smartphone stores its contact database in a relational database. Your online banking information, your financial history, statements, medical data, and social media are all stored in some form of a database.

- SQL is the primary language used to access and analyze information in databases. So, as a Data Ninja who aspires to work intimately with data, it is paramount to master SQL and RDBMS concepts.

 # Resources Center

Phewwww. That was a lot. Are you still with me? Let's keep it going. Now that you have read this game plan and have gotten your feet wet, I hope you've gained a rich and robust understanding of SQL, RDBMS, and some of the peripheral concepts. I can't emphasize how important these concepts are. It would be near impossible to consider yourself a true Data Ninja and work with data at an enterprise scale without the fundamental concepts of SQL—database, table, basic joins, and filtering syntax—down.

I would recommend that you continue to read and practice your SQL & RDBMS skills. The more you read and practice, the more you are going to learn. Pretty soon, you will be fluent in writing SQL statements to interrogate data.

I have put together the best learning resources that I have come across to help you on your journey. Below you will find links to paid online courses that have spent years developing their videos and courses to really immerse you into the material. If you are not ready to shell out some cash, there are also free courses that have excellent content available.

First, we will look at some of the premium resources that are available to purchase. These resources typically have the most to offer and will carry you further than some of the free resources.

About the icons used below:

You will see this icon on top of the resources that cost money.

You will see this icon on top of the resources that are free.

Lynda.com

Lynda.com is a very popular online education company. They offer thousands of different courses for creative software and business skills. Inside the MYSQL course they have several different skill levels from beginner to advanced depending on your skill level. They offer a 10-day trial period to get started; a perfect way to see if their services are right for you. At the end of the trial you can choose between different levels of payment, from $25 a month to $375 annually. http://www.lynda.com/search?q=sql

Infinite Skills

Infinite Skills was recently purchased by O'Reilly media. They offer 142 training videos on MYSQL. They also have downloadable practical files that help further your skills beyond the videos. I find their website to be a little confusing and counterintuitive, but they do offer good videos that will help you. They offer a $25 monthly fee that includes a mobile app. http://www.infiniteskills.com/training/sql-beyond-the-basics.html

Learn Now Online

Learn Now Online has a wide range of topics from programming and mobile development to SQL. I have never personally used them, but they seem to have a nice set of online videos and options to choose from. They are a little more affordable with options starting at $49 annually. http://www.learnnowonline.com/

Paid premium courses are not for everyone. Maybe you want to dive in a little deeper before you decide to pay to further your skills. Below are some great free online courses:

 Udemy

> Udemy is an online marketplace where experts can create their own courses which can then be offered to the public for free. Each course has a different author and has user reviews so you can decide which course will be best for you.
> http://www.udemy.com/

 Learn Code the Hard Way

> Learn Code the Hard Way offers books on various subjects. They are currently working on an SQL book, but have posted the book online for free while they work on it. You can view the book by chapters. Don't let the name fool you, it is very approachable with easy to understand topics. I am assuming once the book is completed it will be available to purchase from their website.
> http://sql.learncodethehardway.org/

 SQL Server Central

> SQL Server Central is a resource in the Microsoft SQL servers community. It has many DBAs, developers and users, so there's plenty of valuable information here. This is one to keep bookmarked as you continue your career in SQL.
> http://www.sqlservercentral.com/

 SQL Fiddle

> SQL Fiddle allows you to select a database, build a schema, populate the schema, and run queries against it. SQL Fiddle is a great resource for practicing different syntax of SQL and testing your queries.
> http://sqlfiddle.com/

Database Journal

Database Journal is a script library which offers a huge database in an array of subjects. They have articles, news, and tutorials all offered for free. Feel free to post questions and comments in their forum section. They update their databases frequently and have topics that date back to 2010.
http://www.databasejournal.com/scripts/

SQL-Tutorial

SQL-Tutorial has resources for novice users and those who feel they already have a grasp on SQL but want to learn more. They will help you program queries. The information is presented as an eBook you can read through.
http://www.sql-tutorial.ru/

1KeyData SQL

1KeyData SQL is a very nice resource to help you with SQL. They have common SQL commands, functions, constraints, and tables available to access whenever you may need them. They also offer some video tutorials and quizzes to help you along.
http://www.1keydata.com/sql/sql.html

The Schemaverse

The Schemaverse is a space-based strategy game implemented entirely within a PostgreSQL database. Play against other players using raw SQL commands to command your fleet. This is a fun way to keep your skills sharp.
https://schemaverse.com/

SQL Zoo

SQL Zoo is a step-by-step tutorial with live interpreters, allowing access to tables using any of Oracle, SQL server, MYSQL, and PostgreSQL engines. Once you feel ready, they also have online quizzes to help assess your skills.
http://sqlzoo.net/

Tutorials Point

Tutorials Point has tons of free online tutorials and reference manuals. They also offer premium services at a fee. If you decide to pay, you will get premium support and help from an instructor. If you do not wish to pay, their free resources are excellent and will help you from the installation of MYSQL all the way through to importing databases.
http://www.tutorialspoint.com//sql/index.htm

SQLCourse

SQLCourse is an interactive online resource that offers free training. They will get you started with the basics and move you along to more advanced topics. The site is funded by advertisements, so you will have to scroll past some ads while you are reading, but they offer great material all about SQL.
http://www.sqlcourse.com/

W3Schools

W3Schools offers free material to view but they also offer premium services such as certificates. In order to receive a certificate you must pay the premium price of $95 and pass an online test. It has a built-in interpreter in the browser so you can try different queries and see the outcomes.
http://www.w3schools.com/

Sol Tutorials

Sol Tutorials GalaXQL is an interactive SQL tutorial. This is another fun tutorial which takes you on a journey into outer space while writing SQL code. The site was created by Kari Komppa. It is totally nonprofit and has sparse advertising, so an enjoyable resource all around. http://sol.gfxile.net/galaxql.html

These are all great online resources to use on your journey to mastering SQL & RDBMS concepts. But sometimes you need to give your eyes a rest from the screen and turn to a physical book. Holding a book and turning the pages has always been my favorite way to learn. There is something about highlighting and underlining key points in the book that just seems to help me remember.

I have collected some of my favorite titles and created a small list below. These titles can be found anywhere that sells computer reference titles:

SQL in 10 minutes

Author: Ben Forta
Published by: Sams Publishing
SBN-13: 978-0672336072

Learning SQL

Author: Alan Beaulieu
Published by: O'Reilly Media
ISBN-13: 978-059652083

SQL Cookbook

Author: Anthony Molinaro
Published by: O'Reilly Media
ISBN-13: 978-0596009762

SQL Queries for Mere Mortals: A Hands-On Guide to Data Manipulation in SQL (3rd Edition)

> Author: John Viescas
> Published by: Addison-Wesley Professional
> ISBN-13: 978-0321992475

 Head First SQL

> Author: Lynn Beighley
> Published by: O'Reilly Media
> ISBN-13: 978-0596526849

It is important to keep learning and using what you've learned. You will only get more proficient as time goes on, so keep fine tuning your skills and never give up.

 # Key NINJA Lessons

✓ Gain familiarity and proficiency in using SQL to interrogate data in databases.

✓ Understand Relational Database Management Systems (RDBMS), the players in the market, and how they work to store and manage data at the fundamental level.

✓ Even better, go beyond SQL into the NoSQL (Not Only SQL). NoSQL is gaining popularity and warrants some attention as well. Make it a point to read up about it, gain an elementary understanding of NoSQL databases, and also understand why the trend is moving in that direction.

Tame Data Integration & Warehousing

> Q: Why did the dimension take all day to take off its suit and put on a pair of jeans?
> A: It was a slowly-changing dimension.

Motivation

In the first part of the game plan, we addressed the importance of MS Excel for data analytics. The second part addressed the need for leveraging SQL & RDBMS systems to do more analytics beyond MS Excel. In this third part of the 5-point game plan, we will explore the challenges of working with huge datasets and the need to adequately move and store them in data warehouses.

You should recall I mentioned the limitations of MS Excel as an enterprise analytical tool. Using Excel for enterprise data analytics projects poses some serious challenges, especially relating to privacy, data redundancy, and concurrency issues that arise when users retain their own personal copies of sensitive corporate data on the personal computers and laptops. Because of these challenges with using Excel spreadsheets, companies often find themselves needing more robust, enterprise-scale tools to help out.

The solution that comes to the rescue when companies are challenged with the need to move and store huge volumes of data falls broadly into the field of *data warehousing (DWH)*. The process of moving data into DWH or any data storage systems within organizations is called *data integration (ETL)*. In this chapter, we will discuss why having skills in both DWH and ETL are essential to a Data Ninja, and as always, provide valuable links and resources at the end to get you started building your Ninja skills in this area.

Numbers have an important story to tell. They rely on you to give them a clear and convincing voice.
~Stephen Few

What Is Data Warehouse (DWH)

Many organizations today have a data warehouse of one form or another. Data warehouses serve many purposes within organizations. But at a basic level, a data warehouse is defined as a massive database typically housed on either a cluster of servers, a miniframe, or mainframe computer serving as a centralized repository of all data generated by all departments and units of a large organization.

The term Data Warehouse (DWH) was coined by W. H. Inmon, a prominent figure in the field of data warehousing. A DWH consolidates data from a variety of sources in one centralized location and is typically designed to support Business Intelligence processes, along with strategic and tactical decision making.

Data Warehousing Defined

> Data warehousing allows a company or organization to create a consolidated view of its enterprise data, optimized for reporting and analysis. Basically, a data warehouse is an aggregated, sometimes summarized copy of transaction and non-transaction data specifically structured for dynamic queries and fast, efficient business analytics.
>
> (InformationBuilders)

With all the company's data available in one location, i.e. the data warehouse, a company can provide data consumers with a coherent picture of the business at any point in time.

Why Is The Data Warehouse Important

Data warehousing is important because it allows for the simplification of data extracted from heterogeneous production data sources. Data warehouses allow for efficient queries when combing through data from multiple sources.

Data Warehouse Architecture

In data warehousing, data is extracted from heterogeneous production data sources as they are generated, and loaded to a common data storage, making it simpler and more efficient to run queries.

The diagram below captures the complete architecture of an end-to-end data warehousing solution within a company.

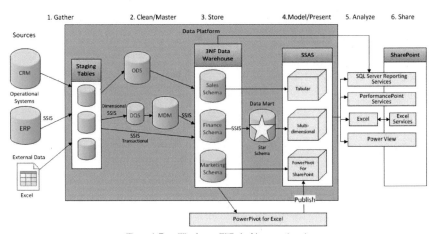

Figure 6, Data Warehouse ETL Architecture. (serra)

From the image illustration above, we see data coming in from various data sources, including CRM, ERP, and any other data sources within the company. These incoming data sources get cleansed in staging areas, and are stored in the DWH. From the DWH, end user applications such as Excel, Microsoft Stack (SQL Server, SSIS, SSRS, and SSAS), Oracle OBIE, and Scribe can all access and consume the data directly.

Data Modeling

A data model is a set of data specifications and related diagrams that reflect data requirements and designs. When you talk about DWH, dimensional modeling usually comes to mind. A **dimensional model** is a database structure that is optimized for online queries and Data Warehousing tools. It is comprised of "fact" and "dimension" tables. A fact is a numeric value that a business wishes to count or sum. A **dimension** is essentially an entry point for getting at the facts.

Given that most data warehouses today follow the dimensional model pattern, an understanding of dimensional data modelling concepts is crucial to learn as a Data Ninja.

Beyond dimensional modelling, there are more modeling techniques and concepts you should be familiar with, including the following: conceptual modeling, enterprise modeling, logical models, physical models, entity-relationship models, canonical data models, ontologies, taxonomies, non-relational models, semantic modeling, ORM, and UML.

ETL And Data Integration

Now that we've talked all about DWH, the big question to ask is "How does data get into the DWH in the first place?" As companies deal with terabytes and petabytes, it's safe to assume that the data won't be residing on some analyst's personal machine, and that the data needs to be moved from point A to B or C or D or E, and additive or deductive transformations and cleansing need to happen on the data along the way. All of these tasks form an entire field of its own called Data Integration, more commonly referred to as ETL (Extract Transform Load), or more recently, ELT (Extract Load Transform).

As a Data Ninja tasked with processing a company's data, you can't just rely on email attachments or thumb drives alone to move this data around. Often, these data would be coming from many different sources and destination. Point of sale systems, CRM systems, ERP systems, customer call logs, website logs, Clickstream, you name it. All these data need to be accessed, moved, cleansed, and transformed in order to bring it to the DWH.

This is where ETL comes into play. ETL is a specialized field where individuals leverage tools like Talend, SSIS, Datastage, Ab Initio, and Scribe to access and move data around an organization.

ETL Tools and Providers

There are many ETL tools and providers in the market, some open sourced and some proprietary. Your company may or may not be using any of the tools on the list, but it's a good starting point to get an understanding of what options are out there. Bitly links have also been included to the main sites if you are interested in further investigation.

Commercial ETL Tools

- IBM Infosphere DataStage
- Informatica PowerCenter
- Oracle Data Integrator (ODI)
- SAS ETL Studio

- Business Objects Data Integrator (BODI)
- Microsoft SQL Server Integration Services (SSIS)
- Ab Initio
- Talend Data Integrator (Enterprise)

Commercial ETL Tools

- Talend - Talend Open Studio
- Pentaho Data Integration (Kettle)
- CloverETL
- Jasper ETL
- Embarcadero Technologies - DT/Studio
- Sybase - Data Integrated Suite ETL

Clearly, ETL tools have their place in today's data-driven enterprises. The ETL process pulls data out of the source, makes changes according to requirements, and then loads the transformed data into a database. ETL platforms that are available in the market save money as well as time to a great extent. Some of them are licensed commercial tools and few are open sourced ones. Using ETL tools makes the data management task much easier and simultaneously improves data warehousing. As we've seen from above, when it comes to choosing the right ETL tool, you have several options.

Some Key Data Warehouse Definitions and Concepts

- **Data Warehouse:** The queryable source of data in the enterprise.

- **Data Mart:** A logical subset of the complete data warehouse.

- **Operational Data Store (ODS):** The point of data integration for operational systems.

- **Metadata Database:** All of the information in the data warehouse environment that is not the actual data itself. It is centrally maintained and stored.

- **Entity Relationship Models (ER):** Entity relationship modeling is a logical design technique that shows the relationship between data.

- **Dimensional Models:** Dimensional modeling is the name of a logical design technique used for data warehouses. Every dimensional model is composed of a "fact" table and a set of "dimension" tables.

- **Facts:** A fact is an event that happened or that has been measured, usually captured as a number, e.g. a single sale of a product to a consumer or the total amount of sales in a specific month.

- **Dimensions:** A dimension relates to facts and contains attributes that can be used to add qualitative information to the numeric information contained in facts. E.g. a dimension can be a list of products or customers.

- **OLAP:** Online Analytical Processing. Online analysis of transactional data. OLAP tools enable users to analyze different dimensions of multidimensional data.

- **OLTP:** Online Transaction Processing. This is a class of information systems that facilitate and manage transaction-oriented applications, typically for data entry and retrieval transaction processing.

- **ETL:** The acronym for the Extract, Transform, and Load process—data integration. ETL processes retrieve data from operational systems and pre-processes it for further analysis using reporting and analytics tools. It's also the ETL process that is responsible for feeding a data warehouse with data.

Summary

Alright, we've gone through a lot. Is your plate getting full and your head spinning from all these terms and concepts? Maybe so. But trust me, it's worth it. I know data warehousing and ETL can be a bit daunting and intimidating once you first get exposed to them. But in my experience, nothing shatters fear or intimidation like competency. Being a Data Warehouse Developer or ETL Developer are lucrative fields in and of themselves.

According to MarketsandMarkets, "The data integration market is expected to grow from $6.44 billion in 2017 to $12.24 billion by 2022, at a compound annual growth rate (CAGR) of 13.7 percent." These are extremely promising figures, and there are people taking home 100K+ salaries doing ETL (data integration) and data warehousing. That could be you.

Resources Center

Below are resources to help you further your knowledge and understanding. Leverage these resources to get started. I'm a firm believer in going beyond theory and actually trying things out for yourself. It's said, he who reads learns, but he who practices knows. You don't just want to be a learner. Strive to know these concepts by practice.

Here is a small project for you to practice with. See if you can build a small data warehouse for yourself. Try using some of the ETL integration tools mentioned in this chapter to integrate some publicly available datasets into your data warehouse. Use a free database like MySQL and a free ETL tool like Talend Open Studio to access data and load your data warehouse. Wouldn't that be a fun project to try!

If you were to build your own data warehouse to practice, you'd inevitably build your confidence. And even if you don't want to take the skills further and make a career out of it, at least you'd have a project to include in your profile to showcase your competency or exposure to these topics. Whatever your aims, use these resources and go for it!

About the icons used below:

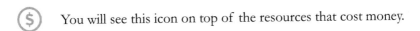

You will see this icon on top of the resources that cost money.

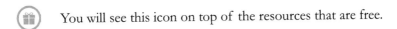

You will see this icon on top of the resources that are free.

The Data Warehousing Information Center

The Data Warehousing Center is a vast collection of essays and articles about everything data warehousing. The site is geared towards someone who is just getting started with data warehouses.
http://www.dwinfocenter.org/getstart.html

Tutorials Point

I've listed Tutorials Point elsewhere because they offer so many great resources. This includes some great tools for learning more about data warehouses. Before you start with them, you should have a basic understanding of database concepts such as schema, ER models, and SQL.
http://www.tutorialspoint.com/dwh/

Learning Data Modeling

Learning Data Modeling focuses on the concepts of data warehouses. It is geared towards the novice user and offers guides and picture graphs to help you understand their concepts. The site is relatively small but has some good articles.
http://www.learndatamodeling.com/

1KeyData

Another site that you will see throughout this book, 1KeyData has an impressive collection of tutorials and resources. 1KeyData is not focused explicitly on beginners, but it tries to bring those with a working understanding to a higher-level of understanding. You will learn about the tools needed to implement a data warehouse, the steps needed to fulfill your needs, and the concepts that cover data warehouses.
http://www.1keydata.com/datawarehousing/datawarehouse.html

Why Learning Data Warehousing Still Matters

This is a great article about why you should learn about data warehouses. It does not offer guides or tutorials but will keep you motivated if you start to lose faith in the importance of learning about data warehouses. https://infocus.emc.com/william_schmarzo/why-learning-data-warehousing-still-matters/

Data Warehousing: Academic Tutorials

Academic Tutorials totes the slogan of "Quick and Easy Learning." They want you to get in and get out quickly while packing as much information as possible. Their tutorials go over pretty much everything you need to know about data warehouses. The site is not very user-friendly and a bit scattered, but if you can figure out how to navigate through the site you will be heavenly rewarded. http://www.academictutorials.com/data-warehousing/data-warehousing-introduction.asp

Lynda

Academic Tutorials totes the slogan of "Quick and Easy Learning." They want you to get in and get out quickly while packing as much information as possible. Their tutorials go over pretty much everything you need to know about data warehouses. The site is not very user-friendly and a bit scattered, but if you can figure out how to navigate through the site you will be heavenly rewarded. http://www.academictutorials.com/data-warehousing/data-warehousing-introduction.asp

Data Modeling 101

Data Modeling 101 has some great picture graphs that easily layout the information you need. The resources provided are limited but if you read through their pages you will pick up some good lessons and well-thought-out information.
http://agiledata.org/essays/bestPractices.html

 Wikipedia

A lot of people shy away from Wikipedia, but when it comes to tech-related information it is usually a good place to start. They can lay out what it is in plain English without relying on tech jargon. They also have many credible links that will help you find good information. It is definitely worth checking out.
https://www.wikipedia.org/

Along with the web-based resources, I highly recommend Ralph Kimball's book *The Data Warehouse Toolkit*. It is a leading authoritative guide on data warehousing—almost like the DWH Bible. In its second edition, *The Data Warehouse Toolkit* has developed into the most comprehensive collection of work on dimensional modeling for data warehousing. A must read if you want to fully understand data warehousing as well as ETL.

 The Data Warehouse Toolkit

Author: Ralph Kimball
Published by: Wiley
ISBN-13: 978-0471200246

Key NINJA Lessons

✓ Data warehousing and ETL concepts are vital to learn as they provide the full picture of data through its life cycle—from creation, to movement, to storage, and finally to consumption.

✓ The data warehouse provides an environment separate from the operational systems and is completely designed for decision-support, analytical-reporting, ad-hoc queries, and data mining.

✓ ETL integration allows you to access any data, ingest, transform, and serve up the data into data warehouses or other consuming applications within companies.

4

Pickup Coding

Q: "What's the
object-oriented
way to become
wealthy?"
A: Inheritance

Motivation

"Computer programming is quickly becoming an essential career skill. Learning to code is a fantastic opportunity equalizer—if you're good at it, it can help you achieve your dreams."
~ *Cory Booker, U.S. Senator, New Jersey*

Alright, let the fun begin. I know this is what you've been waiting for. The chapter on *coding*. I must admit, I was a bit reticent about using the word "coding" to name this chapter. In my experience, coding has a notorious tendency for scaring people off.

Using an analogy from famed Author Dan Ariely, he says coding is like teenage sex: *everyone talks about it, nobody really knows how to do it, everyone thinks everyone else is doing it, so everyone claims they are doing it.*

These days, and largely due to media portrayal, it seems coding is an endeavor reserved solely for the high IQ elite amongst us. While coding is more demanding than some of the other concepts discussed so far, it would be misleading to say it's hard or inaccessible.

In this chapter, not only will I talk about coding and why it's an essential skill warranting its place in the Data Ninja game plan, I'd also be providing you with ample resources and links to get started learning to write code and becoming a programmer.

Computers and Coding

"To be prepared for the demands of the 21st century—and to take advantage of its opportunities—it is essential that more of our students today learn basic computer programming skills, no matter what field of work they want to pursue."
~Todd Park, Former U.S. Chief Technology Officer

Computers are a critical component of our lives today. They are so ubiquitous, we don't even notice how crucial they are. Most things we interact with in the world today are run directly or indirectly by computer systems. As a result, it's crucial for everyone, young and old, to at least understand the basics of these computer systems and the programming that makes them work.

Bill Gates and Mark Zuckerberg recently donated 10 million dollars to Code.org, a non-profit that believes that, "every student in every school should have the opportunity to learn computer programming," and that, "computer science should be a part of the core curriculum."

(NewYorker)

What Is Coding

In general, coding (programming) is defined as the vocabulary and set of grammatical rules for instructing a computer to perform specific tasks.

Programming is highly detailed work, and usually involves fluency in several languages. When working on a programming project, some of them can be short and require only a few days of coding, or they can be very long, involving upward of years to write.

> Programming is the process of designing, writing, testing, debugging, and maintaining the source code of computer programs. This code can be written in a variety of computer programming languages. Some of these languages include Java, C, and Python. Computer code is a collection of typed words that the computer can clearly understand. Just as a human translator might translate from the English language to Spanish, the computer interprets these words as ones and zeros. We as humans use programming languages, instead of writing directly in ones and zeros, so we can easily write and understand the computer code and can organize it. We can think of the different lines of our code as being individual instructions that we give to the computer. The computer follows these instructions explicitly to execute our written code.

(EarSketch)

Why Learn How To Code

> **You Can Play God**
>
> When you program, you are a creator. You go from a blank text file to a working program with nothing to limit you but your imagination (and maybe some issues like how long your program takes to run). Programming is like having access to the absolute best set of legos in the world in almost unlimited qualities. Even better, you can get all of your building materials completely for free (once you own a computer) on the internet. Amazing!

It's also great fun to see someone using something that you made. Your ability to improve your life and the lives of your friends and family is limited only by your ideas once you can take full control of your computer. Moreover, your work can be extremely high quality because the limiting factor is not manual dexterity or other non-mental attributes. If you can understand a programming technique, you can implement and use it.

(Cprogramming.com)

"Whether you want to uncover the secrets of the universe, or you just want to pursue a career in the 21st century, basic computer programming is an essential skill to learn."
~ Stephen Hawking, Theoretical Physicist, Cosmologist, Author

What Experts Say About the Mastery of Programming Skills

Coding isn't particularly easy to learn but that's exactly why it's so valuable. Even if you have no plans to become a software developer, spend a few weeks or months learning to code and I can guarantee it will sharpen your ability to troubleshoot and solve problems.
(DIY Genius)

A deep understanding of programming, in particular the notions of successive decomposition as a mode of analysis and debugging of trial solutions, results in significant educational benefits in many domains of discourse, including those unrelated to computers and information technology per se.
(Seymour Papert, in "Mindstorms")

It has often been said that a person does not really understand something until he teaches it to someone else. Actually, a person does not really understand something until after teaching it to a computer, i.e., express it as an algorithm.
(Donald Knuth, in "American Mathematical Monthly," 81)

Computers are not sycophants and won't make enthusiastic noises to ensure their promotion or camouflage what they don't know. What you get is what you said.
(James P. Hogan in "Mind Matters")

"I think everybody in this country should learn how to program a computer because it teaches you how to think."
(Steve Jobs)

When you learn to read, you can then read to learn. And it's same the thing with coding: If you learn to code, you can then code to learn.

(Mitch Resnick)

Coding (programming) is not a goal. It's a means to an end. It's a tool for solving problems. Learning to program teaches computational thinking which helps people tackle large problems by breaking them down into a sequence of smaller, more manageable problems.

No One Was Born an Expert

As you work with data and mature within the data analytics space, inevitably you will progress from working with small data in spreadsheets to crunching Big Data with tools like Hadoop, Mapreduce, Spark and then maybe onto being a data scientist building machine learning models in Python, Scala or R. In such roles, the need for programming is not only essential, it's a prerequisite.

That said, programming itself doesn't have to be complex or scary. No one was born an "expert" programmer. Everyone who programs today was a beginner at some point in their life. So, start small and keep climbing day by day.

Starting for you can be as simple as creating simple routines in Java, or Shell scripts, or workflows to automate mundane tasks such as moving files, searching folders, merging datasets, creating new datasets, de-duplicating datasets, standardizing datasets, and more.

Then climb your way up the ladder by continuously practicing and developing your skills in more advanced areas like AI, machine learning, deep learning and quantum computing. But to get to those advanced areas, you have to start.

"A journey of a thousand miles begins with a single step." ~ Lao Tzu

Starting Programming As A Novice

The most common question asked by anybody new to computer programming is "What language is the best to start with?". Many people will tell you to jump straight into it by learning a more advanced language such as C++ or Java, others will tell you to start with a more dated language such as C. In my personal opinion, the best programming language to begin learning is Visual Basic .NET. VB.NET is a really good language to learn for a beginner because it requires no previous experience in programming. The Syntax used in VB.NET is simple and very easy to understand. Learning Visual Basic will give you a basic understanding of how computer programming works and is also really entertaining! Although VB.NET is a good place to start, I would not recommend using it for too long. More advanced languages have a more advanced syntax and spending all of your time using VB.NET could make it harder to move onto the more advanced languages in the future.

Although every programming language has a different syntax, most programming languages are similar. The first language that you learn will be the hardest language that you learn because the concept will be new to you. After learning your first language, you will have an understanding of how computer programming works and that will help you a lot when it comes to learning other languages. If you choose a language such as C++ with a more complicated syntax then it is going to be very confusing and hard for you to understand if you do not have any prior experience. The first language that you choose to learn is completely your choice, but we strongly recommend that you begin with VB.NET.

(HowTo)

As the excerpt from the Howtostartprogramming.com article explains, the first step to programming may entail choosing a language and then writing a simple "Hello, World!" program. It's that simple.

From there, you can progress to understanding more complex concepts, such as language syntax, operators, loops, iterations, conditionals, variables and assignments, data types, flow controls and arrays.

With the simpler concepts mastered in a programming language, you can then progress to other programming concepts such as classes, objects, methods, instances and instantiation. Eventually you can move on to more advanced concepts like threads, concurrency, and more.

"Whether we're fighting climate change or going to space, everything is moved forward by computers, and we don't have enough people who can code. Teaching young people to code early on can help build skills and confidence and energize the classroom with learning-by-doing opportunities."
~ Richard Branson, Founder, Virgin Group

Practice Makes Perfect

I must admit that getting into programming can be a challenge and poses a serious learning curve for newcomers. But I would encourage anyone looking to take that step to not be intimidated by the process.

The one important thing I've come to realize is that when learning to program, as with any other thing we learn in life, we don't start as experts. It takes practice, courage, determination and then some *more* practice in order to succeed. I wish I could say it otherwise, but there is simply no way of getting around *practice*. So, get out there and start practicing.

Recipe for Programming Success

* Get **interested** in programming, and do some because it is fun. Make sure that it keeps being enough fun so that you will be willing to put in your ten years/10,000 hours.
* **Program.** The best kind of learning is learning by doing. To put it more technically, "the maximal level of performance for individuals in a given domain is not attained automatically as a function of extended experience, but the level of performance can be increased even by highly experienced individuals as a result of deliberate efforts to improve," (p. 366) and, "the most effective learning requires a well-defined task with an appropriate difficulty level for the particular individual, informative feedback, and opportunities for repetition and corrections of errors," (p. 20-21). The book *Cognition in Practice: Mind, Mathematics, and Culture in Everyday Life* is an interesting reference for this viewpoint.

- **Talk with** other programmers and read other programs. This is more important than any book or training course.

- If you want, put in four years at a **college** (or more at a graduate school). This will give you access to some jobs that require credentials, and it will give you a deeper understanding of the field, but if you don't enjoy school, you can (with some dedication) get similar experience on your own or on the job. In any case, book learning alone won't be enough. "Computer science education cannot make anybody an expert programmer any more than studying brushes and pigment can make somebody an expert painter" says Eric Raymond, author of *The New Hacker's Dictionary*. One of the best programmers I ever hired had only a High School degree; he's produced a lot of great software, has his own news group, and made enough in stock options to buy his own nightclub.

- Work on **projects with** other programmers. Be the best programmer on some projects; be the worst on some others. When you're the best, you get to test your abilities to lead a project, and to inspire others with your vision. When you're the worst, you learn what the masters do, and you learn what they don't like to do (because they make you do it for them).

- Work on **projects** *after* other programmers. Understand a program written by someone else. See what it takes to understand and fix it when the original programmers are not around. Think about how to design your programs to make it easier for those who will maintain them after you.

- Learn at least a half dozen **programming languages.** Include one language that emphasizes class abstractions (e.g. Java, C++), one that emphasizes functional abstraction (e.g. Lisp, ML, Haskell), one that supports syntactic abstraction (e.g. Lisp), one that supports declarative specifications (e.g. Prolog, C++ templates), and one that emphasizes parallelism (e.g. Clojure, Go).

(Norvig)

Which Programming Languages Should I Learn?

"No one in the brief history of computing has ever written a piece of perfect software. It's unlikely that you'll be the first." ~ *Andy Hunt*

Given that this chapter is ultimately about the importance of learning how to program as a Data Ninja, I've pulled together survey results done by Kdnuggets for the popular programming languages in the industry to show how they all stack up in terms of popularity.

Realize that not all programming languages are created equal in terms of functionality and adoption. So use this as a guide to see which ones are used the most. That should inform you on which ones to start learning first.

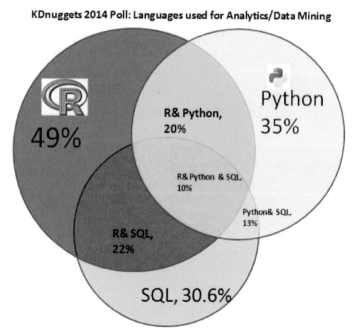

Figure 7, Four main languages for Analytics, Data Mining, Data Science. (kdnuggets)

Which programming/statistics languages you used for analytics / data mining in the past 12 months?[579 voters]

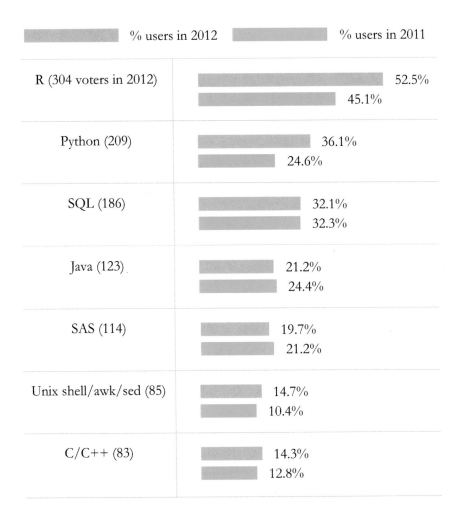

% users in 2012   % users in 2011

R (304 voters in 2012)
52.5%
45.1%

Python (209)
36.1%
24.6%

SQL (186)
32.1%
32.3%

Java (123)
21.2%
24.4%

SAS (114)
19.7%
21.2%

Unix shell/awk/sed (85)
14.7%
10.4%

C/C++ (83)
14.3%
12.8%

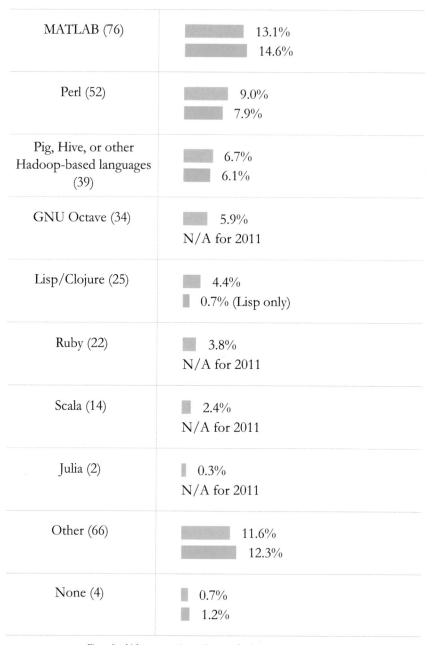

MATLAB (76)	13.1%
	14.6%
Perl (52)	9.0%
	7.9%
Pig, Hive, or other Hadoop-based languages (39)	6.7%
	6.1%
GNU Octave (34)	5.9%
	N/A for 2011
Lisp/Clojure (25)	4.4%
	0.7% (Lisp only)
Ruby (22)	3.8%
	N/A for 2011
Scala (14)	2.4%
	N/A for 2011
Julia (2)	0.3%
	N/A for 2011
Other (66)	11.6%
	12.3%
None (4)	0.7%
	1.2%

Figure 8, which programming tools to use for data analysis. (kdnuggets)

Don't Boil The Ocean

"My success, part of it certainly, is that I have focused in on a few things."
~Bill Gates

Being a programmer is no easy feat. Programming requires a very rich and diverse set of skills to master, and there are many programming languages and concepts out there one can potentially learn.

They say variety is the spice of life, but we all know too much spice in a meal makes it taste bad. As an up-and-coming programmer, knowing how to navigate and deal with the variety ahead of you is just as important as any program you'd actually get to write.

What do I mean by this? I mean you have to FOCUS and PRIORITIZE. Plain and simple! Don't take this game plan of learning how to program as meaning, "learn how to code in every programming language out there." That simply isn't possible and doesn't make sense to do. When starting out as a fledgling programmer, pick two or three of the top languages and focus on them.

As you do so, realize that the main thing needed at this stage is an understanding of several key concepts and how to apply those concepts to solve business problems, as opposed to getting locked down in a particular language or syntax. Once you have mastered the fundamental concepts of programming (e.g. data structures, loops, conditionals) with the top 3 languages you've selected, you can then apply these same concepts to solve specific business problems for companies, regardless of which programming language you use.

The language syntax might change across languages, but programming concepts themselves don't change. So, once you know programming in one language, it's extremely easy to apply it to any other language. And even if the syntax is different, a quick Google search or online articles would give you the exact syntax needed.

> Comparing programming to some physical tasks, programming does not require some innate talent or skill, like gymnastics or painting or singing. You don't have to be strong or coordinated or graceful or have perfect pitch. Programming does, however, require care and craftsmanship, like carpentry or metalworking. If you've ever taken a shop class, you may remember that some students seemed to be able to turn out beautiful projects effortlessly, while other students were all thumbs and made the exact mistakes that the teacher told them not to make. What distinguished the successful students was not that they were better or smarter, but just that they paid more attention to what was going on and were more careful and deliberate about what they were doing.
>
> (Eskimo)

The Gateway To Broader Learning

"Every great developer you know got there by solving problems they were unqualified to solve until they actually did it."
~ Patrick McKenzie

Programming can be hard and time-consuming. So, having a strong "why" is paramount to ensure you stick with the process of mastery. Here, I'll attempt to give you that "why" and make the case even stronger for learning to program.

If you take nothing else from this book, I hope you take away this point. Realize that the goal of learning to program is not to label yourself as a "programmer."

Mitchel Resnick of MIT media labs put it rightly when he said coding is a gateway to broader learning. Once you have invested and mastered programming, it will provide you with the means to think creatively, reason systematically, and work collaboratively to solve countless other problems in your personal and professional life.

Remember that in the same way we learn to read so we can read to learn, you learn to code so you can code to learn. This is an exciting proposition, and that is why learning to code or read code is highly recommended, and will help you thrive as a Data Ninja.

> Good coders are a special breed of persistent problem-solvers who are addicted to the small victories that come along a long path of trial and error. Learning how to program is very rewarding, but it can also be a frustrating and solitary experience. If you can, get a buddy to work with you along the way. Becoming really good at programming, like anything else, is a matter of sticking with it, trying things out and getting experience as you go.
>
> (Lifehacker)

Programming Humbled Me (My Story)

Woooohoooo! You made it successfully through this chapter. Bravo! And YES, I know, the idea of writing code is scary to most people, partly due to misinformation and lack of a warm introduction to the concepts. It wasn't easy for me when I started learning how to code in college. The first language I ever learned to code in was Java, and believe it or not, the first C grade I ever got in my life was in that Java 101 course, Introduction to Programming. I remember it vividly because it scared me to my bones having a "C" grade in programming since I enrolled in college to be a Computer Science major.

Prior to that, I was used to being in the top percentile of my classes throughout high school. So, coming to the USA and receiving that "C" grade in my very first semester was a truly traumatic and humbling experience.

But you know what, I didn't give up. I didn't switch majors or something like that. I just kept pushing and pushing. My classmates would do their homework in under one hour and I'd spend five hours doing mine in the library. The library was my home. All my college professors in my programming classes know and remember me because I was that student who was always in their offices with questions. I reckoned there was no shame in learning. And so, if something didn't make sense to me, I'd ask.

You can get away with being cocky in other areas of life, but not when it comes to learning. My humility and persistence paid off, and today, I can confidently hold my ground in many different programming languages.

I'm sharing my story not to draw sympathy from you, but in hopes of INSPIRING you. If I can go through programming and master it, so can you. The path isn't always easy, but it's worth it. All you have to do is persevere and keep practicing every single day.

To help you on that journey of practice and mastery, I've curated and provided a list of great resources. These resources and the accompanying discussions provided in this game plan will help you get started in programming.

But again, and I say this for the thousandth time (because it's that important): it is *imperative* that you practice your new skills every day. Programming, of course, is like learning a spoken language. Like learning any spoken language for the first time, you can't just read books and be good. You've got to practice frequently to remain fluent.

Best Way To Practice

"Talk is cheap. Show me the code."
~ Linus Torvalds

The best way to practice I've seen is by finding and working on a project. Pick any project, pick your favorite programming language, and start working on it. Seriously, stop reading, and just start!

If you're a student, you could write a program to solve your math homework. It's more interesting than doing sums manually or using MS Excel. If math isn't your thing, you might enjoy making a flashcard program or a quiz to help with your studies. If your area of study is more artistic, maybe try to make your own weight conversion tool, a Rock, Paper, Scissors game, or code a chess game. Chess is a game as old as time and has always followed the same rules. The logic of chess matches up very nicely with the same logic you would use to program a game. If you're really stumped for programming ideas, try making something generic like a calculator or to-do list manager.

When you encounter problems while programming, you will then know what you're missing and what you need to learn more about. But if you're just focused on reading books, you'll find yourself stuck in a rut. Why? Not because you're not smart enough to get the concepts, but because they are not sticking to the brain the same way they would if you practiced.

"Pushing our self [sic] past our boundaries of limitation and extreme, sometimes to something that knocks off our comfort zone, it creates new neural pathways within our brain. We become smarter, wiser, gain more clarity, our life becomes more fulfilling. Only because we have a totally new experience. We get a new brain with that. Neuroplasticity."
~ Angie Karan

So, let me ask you: what project will you take on to build and practice with your favorite programming language? I hope it's something that gets you really excited. Once you've built it, be sure to pull a few friends or colleagues together and demo it to them. There is nothing more fascinating that creating something out of your own imagination that is tangible and actually works. That's the magic of programming.

To help you get started on your programming journey, below are some of my favorite list of curated resources:

Resources Center

About the icons used below:

$ You will see this icon on top of the resources that cost money.

You will see this icon on top of the resources that are free.

Codecademy

Codecademy is arguably the most well-known website on this list for learning to program online. They offer courses in Web Fundamentals, PHP, JavaScript, jQuery, Python, Ruby, and APIs. You can track your progress and learn interactively. The site is well put together and is a great place to start.
http://www.codecademy.com/

EdX

EdX connects students with the highest quality education through their institutional partners. They have a huge catalog of courses in a variety of disciplines, including programming. This is a great resource for anyone trying to expand their knowledge in different sciences.
https://www.edx.org/

Code Avengers

Code Avengers is elegantly designed to make the learning process fun. Every course they offer is strategically designed to entertain while also educating. Code Avengers offers small mini-games after each lesson to help keep your mind relaxed and focused. It is very easy to lose track of time while studying these courses because they are so entertaining. If you have trouble staying focused, Code Avengers is perfect for you.
http://www.codeavengers.com/

ilovecoding

ilovecoding strives to turn beginners into confident developers who can solve any programming task. They offer video tutorials in JavaScript, Angular JS, jQuery, Node JS, and HTML5/CSS. Their courses are designed to be completed within one or two weeks.
https://ilovecoding.org/

Code School

Code School is geared towards those who already have a good understanding of programming and want to go more in-depth. Not only do they offer programming courses, they go over concepts like the industry's best practices to keep you ahead of the curve. They offer courses in Ruby, JavaScript, HTML/CSS, and iOS.
https://www.codeschool.com/

Bento

Bento offers free tutorials and for a fee, they will help you along your path to learn programming. Bento picks the best free tutorials and guides you through them. An interesting site worth checking out, but you will probably want to visit some other sites to get a full experience.
https://www.bento.io/

Khan Academy

The Khan Academy offers a vast array of courses that cover everything from calculus to computer science. People from all around the world use Khan Academy and join together to create an astounding online community.

https://www.khanacademy.org/

Coursera

Coursera is a huge online institution that offers courses from some of the top universities. Coursera is available in five different languages including English, Spanish, French, Italian, and Chinese. This is a great way to get a top-of-the-line education for free.

https://www.coursera.org/

Google University

Google has put together a catalog of online resources to learn an array of things. Google University has just recently gone from their beta stage to being live to the public and is still in its early years. This means it is still growing and will continue to grow. Google is a very reliable company, but since this is not their main area of focus, beginners might find this resource a little unapproachable.

https://developers.google.com/university/

Udacity

Udacity is designed to model universities with online videos led by industry leaders. They have some huge giants helping them make their videos including Google, AT&T, Facebook, Salesforce, and Cloudera. Udacity offers credentials in the form of a "Nanodegree" to give you something to put into your resume.

https://www.udacity.com/

Code Combat

A lot like Code Avengers, Code Combat is designed to teach while the user plays a fun game. It is geared towards beginners and instantly throws you into a game where you are writing code. The people at Code Combat really tried to make this game addicting so you forget you are learning to code while you are playing. It can seem like it's for children, but just because you are an adult doesn't mean you can't have fun while learning.
http://codecombat.com/

 ## The Odin Project

The Odin Project is still in its beta release but everything seems to be running immaculately. The people who started The Odin Project felt there was a hole in the market and they wanted to create something that would fill that hole. They offer resources in web development, Ruby programming, Ruby on Rails, HTML5/CSS3, JavaScript, jQuery, and also offer discussions on how to get hired as a web developer.
http://www.theodinproject.com/

 ## Quakit

Quakit offers free web tutorials, codes, templates, and tools. It's a very friendly site with resources in HTML, CSS, coding, databases, web hosting, and XML. Each category offers many tutorials for you to read through.
http://www.quackit.com/

Saylor Academy

Saylor Academy is a non-profit online academy. They have designed their site after universities. They label their courses just as a college would (e.g. ARTH110). Once you sign up it will feel like you are taking an online class at your local college, however, they are not accredited and you will not receive a diploma. They offer courses in both arts and sciences. This is a great resource for anyone who wants to further their knowledge in any subject, coding included.
https://eportfolio.saylor.org/

Learn Python the Hard Way

I've listed Learn the Hard Way platform elsewhere, but again don't let the name scare you off. Their online books are very approachable, but force you to type every lesson yourself so you cannot take any shortcuts. The only hard part is the self-discipline. The cost of the online book is $29.
http://learnpythonthehardway.org/

Code Mentor

Code Mentor is a unique experience that connects you with real people who specialize in coding. Codementor connects you with experts for instant problem-solving, technical advice, pair programming, and code review. Every mentor sets their own rate so the prices vary from mentor to mentor.
https://www.codementor.io/

Career Foundry

Career Foundry is geared towards beginners with no previous experience. They only offer two courses, web developer and user experience designer.
http://careerfoundry.com/

BaseRails

BaseRails is a project-based learning site. Learn Ruby on Rails along with other web technologies. Rather than simply teaching you code, they will guide you through building specific sites such as review sites, marketplaces, and data collection sites.
https://www.baserails.com/

 Coder Camps

Coder Camps is a very intricate site that offers very good courses. Coder Camps offers courses in .NET, JavaScript, iOS, and HTML/CSS. You can apply for a scholarship to help pay for your tuition. There is a large tuition fee from $9,000 to $12,000, but they offer a deferred payment option where you pay a $1,000 down payment then pay off the rest after completion. It's hard to recommend a site with such a high fee when there are so many great learning resources online with no costs. If you have the money, this site will offer you a lot more than the free sites, but don't worry if you don't have the money. There are some great free sites that I've already listed.
http://www.codercamps.com/

 Code School

Code School is a little less expensive than Coder Camps, but still with some great options. They offer courses in Ruby, JavaScript, HTML/CSS, iOS, Git, and many more languages. Their fee is either $29 a month or $290 annually.
https://www.codeschool.com/

Hack Reactor

Hack Reactor is an online immersive coding program. They have built their program off classroom-based learning. They have sign-ups for their classes and if you miss the signup, you will have to wait for the next one. You will be a student in a class with an instructor who can help you one-on-one if needed.

http://www.hackreactor.com/

Treehouse

The courses at Treehouse are great for the novice programmer. Unlike most of the other sites listed here, Treehouse is project-oriented and will help you prepare for most projects you have planned.

https://teamtreehouse.com/

BLOC

BLOC is an online boot camp with programs in web development, mobile development, and design. BLOC has designed a structured program that is immersive, but still can fit into your busy schedule. They offer a very structured track of courses that vary from 15 hours to 40 hours.

https://www.bloc.io/

Learnable

Learnable offers over 500 video tutorials with unlimited online access to all of them. They offer help in HTML/CSS, JavaScript, PHP, Ruby, Design/UX, Mobile OS, and Workflow. When you subscribe to their service, you'll also gain access to a huge eBook library available online, or you can download them and put them on a tablet device to read them anywhere.

https://learnable.com/

Thinkful

> Thinkful is another mentor-based site that connects you with experts in your field of study and offers one-on-one help. These mentor sites are great if you are working on a project and get stuck. They can look at your code and help you debug the problem.
> https://www.thinkful.com

Below is a list of resources that are aimed towards kids. These resources understand how younger brains work and have designed their courses to be engaging and fun for kids to learn how to code.

 Code.org

> A simple name with extraordinary results. The two Partovi brothers created this non-profit organization to encourage school students to learn computer science. This is a very well-thought-out site that aims to reach the minorities inside the programming world.
> http://code.org

CS Unplugged

CS Unplugged takes a different approach to teaching programming. Rather than having online courses, they offer a free PDF book that is a collection of games, puzzles, cards, and activities that students can use without a computer to learn computational thinking. It won't take someone from beginner to master coder, but it will get kids to start thinking in a way that will set them up for success later in life. You can also purchase a physical book from their partner website for $20. http://csunplugged.org/

Summary

Programming is becoming essential for everyone in the modern world. There are many resources to learn programming and sharpen your skills, and I hope you find the ones that have been included in this game plan to be valuable. Learning to program is like learning a language, and you must practice every day to stay fluent.

Key NINJA Lessons

✓ Get beyond the fear of reading or writing code and start getting familiar with the concepts.

✓ Programming syntax and languages may change, but the programming techniques used to solve particular business problems do not change for the most part.

✓ Remember that in the same way we learn to read so we can read to learn, you learn to code so you can code to learn.

✓ The choice is yours to make. Start simple! Pick a language that suits your needs and practice with it in order to build competence. I'm sorry! There's no easy way to get around the practicing part.

5

Continue Adapting

When the winds of
change blow, some
people build walls
and others build
windmills.
~ Chinese Proverb

Motivation

Alright. You've powered through the previous chapters and made it here. Congrats! This is arguably the most important chapter in this book, so I'm glad you're here. So far, we've covered a lot of rich and exciting topics. I'm sure your head is oozing with information and your Data Ninja skills are sharper than ever before: you now understand Excel, SQL, RDBMS, data warehousing, ETL, programming and more. These are rich and highly sought after skills that takes years to master. But as I've preached all along, don't let the complexity of these concepts fool you. They are all remarkably simple. If you just start and continue making progress each day, leveraging the hundreds of links and resources provided thus far, you will succeed as a Data Ninja.

That said, why would I dedicate an entire game plan on "change"? The answer is simple—it's that important! Einstein once said, "the only thing that is constant is change," and nowhere is this more true than in IT or, more specifically, data analytics.

I've been in the field for close to a decade now and hopefully decades more to come. I'm astonished every day by how fast things are changing. Even though I've provided a lot of resources and covered a lot of concepts, be rest assured that all of these can change and become irrelevant within a few years. That's the reality of the beast, and you must be prepared to change and constantly sharpen your skills. Ninjas change and adapt, and so must you! In this chapter, we'll provide a game plan and take a closer look at what change means to you as a Data Ninja.

A Walk Down Memory Lane

"Technological change is not additive; it is ecological. A new technology does not merely add something; it changes everything"."
~ Neil Postman

Looking back twenty years or so on consumer technology, gadgets like cassette tapes, walkmans, and floppy disks were the norm, and every cool kid on the block wanted to own one of these items. But these once "cool" technologies of the 1980s and 1990s bear almost no resemblance to what we have today.

In the same way, technology around us is changing at warp speed. Our jobs and organizations of today probably bear little resemblance to those of a few years ago. Think about it, Facebook didn't even exist in 2003, and now it's everywhere. Uber just came to prominence in 2014. Now, it's on the verge of offering self-driving car rides. We are truly living in exciting and highly fluid times. Let's be daring and even look ahead twenty years from now. Can you imagine what the future will look like? I know I can't. And if you think you can, you're probably fooling yourself. The only thing we can guarantee is that things will have changed and won't be what they are today. As a Data Ninja, you have to develop the skills and competencies to not only survive when things change, but to thrive when they do. This chapter will give you some tips and resources on how to do so.

"Only the wisest and stupidest of men never change."
~Confucius

The Hype Cycle

Making predictions about the future is hard, especially in the data analytics space where change happens almost daily. In the industry, the Gartner Technology Hype Cycle is the leader in making predictions about what technology tools will live or flop in coming years. This is something I pay close attention to see what technologies are winning and which ones are falling behind. The Gartner Hype Cycle is something I highly recommend you pay close attention to. There are many more companies like Gartner with their own versions of the hype cycle on technology tools and trends such as Forrester, IT Central Station, Experts Exchange, Whale Path, TrustRadius, Capterra, Comparz, and IDC. Honorable mentions include Stack Overflow, Reddit and LinkedIn. Regardless of which of these sources you subscribe to, mind you, what they offer are only predictions, not declarations. So, take it for what it's worth.

> *Learning and innovation go hand in hand. The arrogance of success is to think that what you did yesterday will be sufficient for tomorrow.*
> *~William Pollard*

Over time, Gartner has added a comprehensive range of hype cycles covering technology applications like e-commerce, CRM, ERP and Business Intelligence. Many of their predictions are only available to paid subscribers, but Gartner does share some of the broader hype cycles through their blog/ press releases.

Gartner's Hype Cycle for Emerging Technologies Maps the Journey to Digital Business

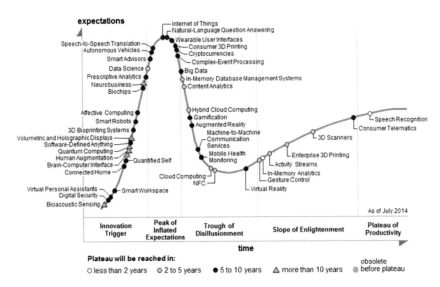

Figure 9: Garter's Hype Cycle (gartner)

In order to come up with these hype cycles, Gartner examines more than 2,000 technologies on their maturity, their business benefits, and their future orientation. The Gartner Hype Cycle is a result of these evaluations and is especially relevant for your game plan because it offers a cross-sectional perspective of those technologies and trends that senior executives, CIOs, innovators, and technology planners should consider in preparation of a strategic technology portfolio.

In their most recent hype cycle (shown above), we see ten big predictions that are definitely worth your attention as a Data Analytics Ninja:

Autonomous 'things'

The evolution of machines (e.g. computers, drones) into self-operating technology.

5G Wireless

Evolved wireless internet that will enable technology such as self-driving cars and factory robots to quickly respond to commands and become a stable part of society.

Augmented reality or virtual reality

Immersive digital experiences with a variety of uses including entertainment and therapy.

3D Printing

Computer-controlled process of solidifying a material (i.e. powder grains, liquid molecules) to create 3D objects. An evolved manufacturing process which is sweeping across many industries.

Edge Computing

Data processing that happens at the "edge" of a network in clusters rather than a centralized cloud. Makes data processing more efficient by decreasing latency and data travel distance.

Artificial Intelligence

Simulated machine intelligence which has found use in many industries. Replaces human labor in fields such as healthcare, military, and the automotive industry.

Cloud Computing

Data and computer resource storage in centralized online locations rather than local servers.

Blockchain

A revolutionary cryptography tool that allows for flawless record-keeping of transactions. It is the foundation of cryptocurrency.

Digital Ethics and Privacy

The growing field of ethics preparing for the moral and social obligations of the near-future where virtually everyone will have personal digital data.

Quantum Computing

Computing based in quantum mechanics rather than binary code. Has the potential to elevate cryptography, search engines, and the scope of computer simulation.

As you can see, the list of technologies on the hype cycle is long. However, I must caution you: don't kill yourself trying to master every single one of them. Doing so would be a futile effort, it simply can't be done! Instead, take a broader approach and acquaint yourself with each of the technologies. Be able to hold a conversation with someone about quantum computing and qubits, blockchain, or deep learning for example, without looking totally ignorant. That's what it takes to succeed.

Once you have the broad perspective down, then it's time to be selective and dive a little deeper. Pick a few of your favorite areas (ideally, one in the top-10 list provided above) and focus on them. For the ones you've selected, strive to understand not only how the technologies work, but understand how they will affect you. Read every single article and book, watch videos, and be familiar with all the opinions out there on the topic. Even better, form your own opinions as well. After all, it's the future, and the best anyone can do is make guesses. And if anyone was going to make guesses about the future, your future, why not be at the dinner table and be part of the conversation?

"One of the greatest challenges in creating a joyful, peaceful and abundant life is taking responsibility for what you do and how you do it. As long as you can blame someone else, be angry with someone else, point a finger at someone else, you are not taking responsibility for your life."
~ Iyanla Vanzant

If you're not at the dinner table, you might as well be on the menu. Don't sit on the sidelines. Be part of the conversation. Educate yourself well enough to make your own predictions. And if you're so inclined, share them with friends, colleagues, or me.

Change Is The Only Constant

"The measure of intelligence is the ability to change" ~ Albert Einstein

As we've discussed throughout this chapter and game plan, we can make informed guesses, but we cannot perfectly predict the future of data analytics. But since history is such a good teacher, I can say for sure that things will change and be different than what we are used to today. Change, inevitable as it is, is a nuanced concept that comes in many flavors and is worth some extra attention. Below, we look at the two main flavors of change you're going to encounter on your journey as a Data Analytics Ninja—evolutions and revolutions.

Evolutionary Changes

Most of us are accustomed to evolutionary changes. They are slow and less noticeable, but still happen. For example, when tools and software products get upgraded, like going from SQL 2000 to SQL 2008 or SQL 2018, it is an evolutionary process. Slowly, new features were added to the base product, and all SQL server professionals had to do was learn the new features as they came. Going from MS Excel 2000 to Excel 2018 is evolutionary change as well. Nothing radically different happens. MS Excel as we know it doesn't change much except for the incremental addition of new features.

The changes that happen in SQL or MS Excel are evolutionary by nature—they come often, move us forward, and we can deal with them through upgrades and by reading a few new books.

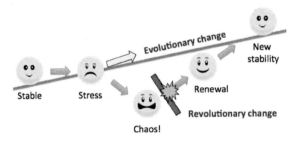

Figure 7: Revolutionary change cycle (Hangthebankers.com)

Revolutionary Changes

Revolutionary changes, on the other hand, are changes that come much less often. But when they do, they fundamentally change the affected industries and rock it from top to bottom. Think about inventions such as paper currency, the light bulb, the automobile, antibiotics, transistors, microprocessors, and more. Without these inventions, society wouldn't be where it is today.

Even in the data analytics space, we see these revolutionary types of changes on the horizon promising to alter how we collect, store, and process data.

Today in the mainstream, we think in terms of databases with tables, rows, and columns when storing data. Tomorrow, databases as we know them may change, replaced by entirely new constructs, forcing us all to eschew what we previously knew and adopt what's new.

Tools like graph databases, NoSQL, Hadoop, Spark, Containers, Serverless and many other products are all at the cutting edge and are radically changing the field of data analytics as we know it. Artificial intelligence, deep learning, and quantum computing are all making significant advances we couldn't even fathom a few years ago. What would the world look like in a future where quantum computing goes mainstream and previously uncrackable codes and cryptography can be cracked in seconds? Today's passwords would become obsolete instantly.

What would happen when the advances we see in deep learning results in machines blowing past the Turing test and bringing us into The Singularity (the point when all the advances in Artificial Intelligence (AI) will lead to machines being smarter than human beings)?

What is a Turing Test?
The Turing Test is named after British mathematician Alan Mathison Turing who is often considered to be the father of modern computer science. In 1950, Turing published an article titled Computing Machinery and Intelligence where he introduced what he believed to be a practical test for assessing computer intelligence.
The Turing test is an interactive test involving three participants—a computer, a human interrogator, and a human participant. It is a blind test where the interrogator asks questions via keyboard and receives answers via display screen on the basis of which he or she has to determine which answers come from the computer and which from the human subject.
According to Alan Turing if a statistically sufficient number of different people play the roles of interrogator and human subject, and, if a sufficient proportion of the interrogators are unable to distinguish the computer from the human being, then the computer is considered an intelligent, thinking entity or AI.
http://www.singularitysymposium.com/turing-test.html

One could go on forever and fill an entire book with these la-la technologies of the future. But no need to belabor the point, as you get it by now. Revolutionary changes are a lot to wrap one's head around, so naturally we might resist adaptation. But doing so would be akin to sticking to horse-drawn wagons in an era of supersonic jet travel. If you take nothing away from the book, please heed my advice to embrace the future with an open mind. Open wide enough so that all the old ideas in your brain are made available to replace. The people who will win in the future are not only the ones who can learn quickly, but the ones who can *unlearn* fast enough to make room for these new concepts to take hold.

I understand any debate about the future is contentious. Some people are pessimistic about the future, but I am an optimist. And if the advances you see today don't inspire you, I don't know what will.

Whether or not these technologies will actually deliver on the hype surrounding them is not a prediction I'm comfortable making. But one way or another, things will change, including the tools and techniques we currently use for data analysis. As a Data Ninja, you've got to not only be comfortable with the tsunami of change that is coming, but be prepared for it.

70/30 Principle

Now that we've looked at the hype cycle and talked a whole lot about the inevitability of change, this section will offer some insights and advice on how to put it into practice and learn (or unlearn) the vital technologies.

I spend a lot of time reading about new technologies and seeing what is out there. Being aware of what is coming is just as important as mastering what you already know.

"Flexibility is a learned mental skill. In today's dynamic world, your effectiveness as a professional depends
on your readiness to adjust quickly to the moments of need or opportunity, adversity, and change."
~ Jennifer Touma

For me it's a 70/30 equation when it comes to flexibility, awareness, learning and investing in mastering emerging technology concepts.

Invest 70% of your time in learning what is happening around the industry today. This is the 2-5-10 year future view of the industry. What technologies are currently hot, and what companies are mainly hiring for? This foresight and skills is what gets you a job and keeps your job short term.

For the long term, spend the remaining 30% of your time investing in what is coming in the future. This is your 15-30-50 year plan. In this case, you're looking at the more exotic and moon-shot type technologies. AI, quantum computing, augmented reality, serverless, blockchain, neurohacking, mass data, nanotech, and so on. Look for technologies that will not just transform but disrupt industries. And then hedge your bets by learning about them and mastering them early on.

Companies might not be looking at these technologies today, but you know there's a chance they'll inevitably come. It's better that you're prepared when they arrive rather than scrambling to play catch-up. That way, you won't be suddenly swept out of a job by a new technology.

Think of all the taxi drivers responding to Uber now. They didn't see it coming, so they're paying the price. As sad as it is to say, many of them will be out of a job soon if they don't adapt. Don't let that be you. Learn to read the tea leaves early on, pick out signs of widespread change, and ready yourself by investing in learning—finding books, following interesting blogs, and more. You can't predict the future or stop change, but at least you can be prepared for it.

"What I try to focus on is not to try to stop the march of technological progress. Instead, I try to run faster."
~ Yuval Noah Harari

Ninja Tip

In his classic work The Art of War, author and military strategist Sun Tzu wrote about the importance of observing signs of the enemy.

In it, he wrote that movement among trees in a forest indicates an advancing enemy brigade, and that dust which rose in a high column indicated the approach of chariots.

In the same token of observing signs, it's important that you find and pay attention to such vital signs in the industry. Identifying incoming chariots of change will help you make critical career decisions early on rather than being late to the game, or losing out entirely.

Summary

Change is constantly around us. Sometimes it is so minute and consistent that we do not notice it, while other times it is so severe and sudden that it bowls us over. As Darwin famously wrote in his book *The Origins of Species*:

> *"It is not the strongest of the species that survives, nor the most intelligent that survives. It is the one that is most adaptable to change."*
> *~ Charles Darwin*

The field of data analytics is constantly changing and no one (including me) can predict which tools or processes will be used five, ten, or twenty years from now. At the very most, all we can do is speculate.

But despite the certainty of change, it should not paralyze or prevent us from being effective Data Ninjas. What it should do is inspire us to adapt to new technologies, tools, and practices the future throws at us.

If you can learn how to stay relatively unaffected by change, handle new technological developments with confidence, unlearn old techniques, and adapt to any curve balls that come your way, you will stand the test of time and truly win in your career.

Below, I've provided a sample of my favorite sites and articles to help you better prepare for change. Bookmark them and visit them daily. It's a lot easier to change when you're ready and willing to do so, rather than change when you are being forced to.

 Resources Center

About the icons used below:

($) You will see this icon on top of the resources that cost money.

(🎁) You will see this icon on top of the resources that are free.

The tech world is a fast-paced, ever-changing living organism. New advancements can make a whole field obsolete overnight. Startup companies are popping up everywhere offering a vast array of innovative products, services, and technologies. It is crucial to read a diverse source of literature and stay on top of how things are changing to keep yourself competitive and relevant.

"How Technology Is Transforming Our Brains"

Published, 2013
http://www.digitaltonto.com/2013/how-technology-is-transforming-our-brains/

 "Top 5 Reasons why software professionals need social skills, too"

Published, 2011
http://www.computertrainingschools.com/articles/importance-of-social-skills-for-tech-professionals.html

 "10 highly valued soft skills for IT pros"

Published, 2013
http://www.techrepublic.com/blog/10-things/10-highly-valued-soft-skills-for-it-pros/

 "7 Simple Ways to Stay Current on Technology"

Published, 2012
http://allthingsadmin.com/administrative-professionals/stay-current-technology/

 "8 Ways to Advance Your Career by Staying Relevant"

Published, 2012
http://www.cio.com/article/2448966/careers-staffing/8-ways-to-advance-your-it-career-by-staying-relevant.html

"6 Ways to Stay Current in Your Field and Advance"

Published, 2010
http://www.personalbrandingblog.com/6-ways-to-stay-current-in-your-field-and-advance/

To stay informed and evolve in the field of data analytics, you need to keep reading and learning new concepts and techniques. In addition to the library of resources we've already provided, below is a list of my favorite tech blogs and websites that are valuable sources of news and updates. Use them to learn and stay informed on technologies, especially relating to general trends within the industry. I have tried to only include sites that have a stable revenue and user base to ensure that they will be around for years to come.

ZDNet

ZDNet was founded in 1991 and acquired by CNET in 2000. ZDNet publishes product reviews, software downloads, news, analysis, and guides.
http://www.zdnet.com/

GIGAOM

Gigaom was created in 2006 by Om Malik. They devote all their efforts into finding the newest and best in tech. News and analysis on web 2.0, startups, gaming, social media, and everything else tech. With over 6.5 million unique visitors every month Gigaom is trying to humanize technology and make it approachable for everyone.
https://gigaom.com/

Mashable

Mashable reports on the importance of digital innovation. With over 42 million unique visitors monthly, Mashable is truly a tech media powerhouse. They report on social media, entertainment, news, startups, and anything else techies are talking about.
http://mashable.com/

Wired

Wired is a full-colored monthly magazine based in the United States. They report on emerging technologies, economics, and politics. Their magazine is full of interesting thought provoking articles that will inspire and amaze. Their website offers free articles and news. They cover absolutely everything any tech-savvy person could care about. Subscribe to their magazine and you'll learn something new every time you pick it up.
http://www.wired.com/

TechCrunch

TechCrunch is one of my favorite tech sites to visit on a daily basis. Like Wired above, they cover almost everything you'll need to stay current in the tech world. They do not limit themselves to tech, as they also delve into politics and worldwide news. The site has grown immensely since its founding in 2005.
http://techcrunch.com/

DataTau

This is the most technical and Big Data-oriented of all the resources listed in this nugget. DataTau is like Hackernews for data science. The simple interface makes the site feel like a handpicked list of articles for Big Data/data scientists. There is often interesting pop-up content as well.
http://www.datatau.com

KDNuggets

> KDnuggets is an online platform on Machine Learning, Data Science, Data Mining, Big Data, Analytics, AI. Software, Jobs, Academia, Meetings, Conferences, Courses, Polls - you name it, they have it all. With over 150,000 unique monthly visitors, and over 70,000 subscribers via email - this is a site you definitely want to bookmark and visit often.
>
> http://www.kdnuggets.com

This list is just the crust of tech-related blogs and sites out there on the web. If you visit any one from the list above, you will discover more blogs and affiliates to follow and expand your knowledge with. Keep searching for new technologies and skills while adding to the wealth of skills you've gained from reading this book.

 # Key NINJA Lessons

✓ Change requires flexibility. The better you are at adapting to change, the greater your chances of being successful.

✓ "Enjoying success requires the ability to adapt. Only by being open to change will you have a true opportunity to get the most from your talent." - Nolan Ryan, Major League Baseball Hall of Famer

✓ Stay curious and adapt. Change is the only thing that will remain constant.

Part 3

Inspiration & Parting Words

> You are very
> powerful,
> provided you
> know how
> powerful you are.
> ~Yogi Bhajan

The Time Is Right

The time is right for you to get in and add value to organizations by working with data. The work done by Data Ninjas, as we have presented throughout this book, employs a lot of tools and techniques which constantly evolve. Many companies increasingly depend on Data Ninjas who can go beyond the basic aspects of crunching numbers or wrangling data to master the subtle nuances of the trade as a whole. These are Ninjas who not only perform analysis, but are equipped to see the big picture and do work in ways that positively affect the bottom line.

"You are very powerful, provided you know how powerful you are."
~Yogi Bhajan

Stuff To Blow Your Mind

The excerpts presented below are the results of work done by real world Data Ninjas. These are only a few stories of high-performing companies that are making the best of the data boom.

IBM
IBM's work has revealed genetic traits of cancer survivors and tracked the source of an E. coli outbreak. It recently aided the influential Washington, D.C.–based think tank Institute for the Study of War by creating a map of terrorist behavior in and around Baghdad during a campaign to free imprisoned Al Qaeda members.

THE WEATHER COMPANY
By analyzing the behavior patterns of its digital and mobile users in 3 million locations worldwide—along with the unique climate data in each locale—the Weather Company has become an advertising powerhouse, letting shampoo brands, for example, target users in a

humid climate with a new anti-frizz product. It's no surprise that more than half of the Weather Company's ad revenue is now generated from its digital operations.

EVOLV

Evolv's data scientists have uncovered several eye-opening correlations: People with two social media accounts perform much higher than those with more or less, and in careers such as call-center work, employees with criminal backgrounds performed better than those with squeaky-clean records. Evolv's sales grew a whopping 150% from Q3 2012 to Q3 2013.

GE

Over the past year, General Electric has taken the lead in tying together what Chairman Jeff Immelt calls, "the physical and analytical worlds." Translation: GE's many machines—everything from power plants to locomotives to hospital equipment—now pump out data about how they're operating. GE's analytics team crunches it, then rejiggers their machines to be more efficient. Even tiny improvements are substantial given the scale: By GE's estimates, data can boost productivity in the U.S. by 1.5%, which over a 20-year period could save enough cash to raise average national incomes by as much as 30%.

(FastCompany)

We can talk technology and geek out all day, but ultimately it's important to step back and understand why this all matters. Businesses rely on you. Lives depend on the work you do. The work you do as a Data Ninja has real world impact and you should be proud of that. If nothing else, I hope reading these stories will inspire you to go out there with the skills, confidence, and gusto to be the best Data Ninja possible.

"Information technology and business are becoming inextricably interwoven. I don't think anybody can talk meaningfully about one without talking about the other."
~Bill Gates

Success Stories

We've spent quite a bit of time talking about why you should become a Data Analytics Ninja and be part of the booming and lucrative field. I've given you a game plan with tons of tips, tricks, and resources to get you started on your journey. Despite all of that, some of you might still be on the fence. Perhaps an excuse is holding you back. Maybe you're asking yourself, "Does any of this advice work? Is it worth following?"

Stop being afraid of what could go wrong, and start being excited about what could go right.
~Tony Robbins

My goal is to shatter those hesitations and share some stories of people who've either implemented this game plan already, or are in the process of doing so and are starting to see massive success as a result.

Victor

Victor immigrated to the USA from Kenya back in 2010. When he arrived, like many other immigrants, he didn't have any experience in IT. But the lack of a technical background didn't stop Victor from dreaming of one day working in IT. For him, the biggest motivator was the pay potential.

In Victor's words, "I know it's good to work for passion. But in my case, reality demands much more than passion. It demands money, and I've got to earn more. You see, where I'm from, it's not just about me. Once you make it to the USA, your responsibility goes far beyond yourself. The paycheck you get needs to stretch to your family, external family, friends, and even friends of friends." From Victor's expression, we can see the need to be more and earn more is always on his mind.

When Victor arrived, he worked at a few odd jobs, then a warehousing gig doing shipping and packing. The pay was ok to get by, but nothing like the 100K+ salary Victor saw when he looked at IT job postings on job sites like Dice.com and Glassdoor.com.

As a result, Victor decided to make the switch. He'd continue his work, but on the side, he'd study technology so he can get in. When Victor first approached me for advice, his goal was to become a Big Data engineer. That seemed to be the gig that paid the most. After discussing with Victor, I gave him all the ins and outs of working as a Big Data engineer based on my experience. More importantly, we talked about the need to have a game plan. So, we sat down and formulated one.

Today, Victor has left the warehouse job far behind. He earns almost double what he used to while working more comfortable hours and having more time to spend with his little daughter and wife. Victor works as a database administrator and ETL developer for the state. He's currently studying Python, understands data warehousing, has taken some Big Data training course, and is well on his way to realizing both the professional aspirations and income potential he's always dreamt of.

Emma

Emma is a very driven individual originally from Liberia. Emma immigrated to the USA at a young age, but still has strong connections to family back in Liberia.

When we first connected, Emma was very high energy. He'd sometimes talk more than he listened, which wasn't necessarily a bad thing. I liked it because I enjoyed all the ideas about his future Emma would throw at me. He wanted to do business, start a website, build some apps, drive Uber, create his own Uber, ship containers, start a cleaning business, buy some rental properties, work in IT, seriously, you name it.

But the only problem he had was not having the capital to realize his dreams. At this time, Emma still worked at a warehouse. He didn't like the hours and the paycheck was long gone before the month ended.

Underneath the jovial disposition, I knew Emma wasn't happy with the situation and wanted a change.

I soon learned Emma was an avid reader. He had a ton of technical books in his home, and he held a Bachelor's and a Master of Business Administration degree (MBA). The MBA alone should have qualified him for some lucrative job somewhere. But that hadn't happened.

So, we took to task formulating a game plan. The first thing was FOCUS. All those business ideas Emma had would have to wait. After all, you can't launch businesses without funds. Plus, I promptly advised him, you can't chase two rabbits at once. You'd end up catching neither. So, we focused solely on his IT dreams to let the rest fall into place. Next was learning the basics. Even though Emma had what seemed like a big degree, Emma was lacking some of the fundamental skills of IT. Covering the basics of things like Excel, ETL, and data warehousing was essential.

Emma took his game plan and became a learning machine. In addition to the books he had amassed, he enrolled in several online courses on YouTube, Udemy, Coursera, and Linda.com and learned as much as he could according to his game plan.

Today, Emma works for a very lucrative company doing data analytics. He earns more and has more time to spend with his beautiful wife who just arrived from Liberia to join him. Even better, he can use his newfound flexible hours to work on his dreams and side businesses without compromise.

Patrick

As you know from the introduction of the book, Patrick's story is inspiring. An immigrant like the first two people covered, Patrick hails from Cameroon. He also serves in the U.S. Army (thank you for your service). In my first interaction with him, Patrick came off as mellow and soft-spoken. But beyond the soft voice, Patrick was a very inquisitive and driven individual. Nothing passed Patrick without him asking questions and being 110% sure.

When Patrick first approached me, he was just months from completing his Master's degree at a very reputable university in the state of Minnesota. He had paid a lot for that program, so I was a little confused as to why, after the completion of an advanced degree in data analytics, he needed me.

So, we got to work. After discussing, I realized that prior to the data analytics Master's program Patrick had taken, he didn't have much background or experience in IT at all. He learned some new and advanced skills through the program, but he struggled to put it all together. This scared him, as he needed a job upon graduation, but wasn't sure where the things he'd learned in school would fit.

As you may recall, we formulated a game plan. Patrick was a clear case of someone who had learned how to fly without first learning how to walk. Patrick could talk advanced concepts in R, Python, and Hadoop, but had very little fundamental understanding of data, ETL, and other basic concepts.

Patrick's game plan didn't involve him learning up. It was learning down. Mastering basic concepts so he can tie all the advanced concepts together.

After a few months of working with Patrick on his game plan, not dissimilar to what has been discussed in this book, Patrick quickly secured a lucrative consulting gig at a major Fortune 500 company earning a 120K+ annual salary—way more than he ever dreamed of. It all came down to his drive and ability to follow a solid game plan.

Everyone's journey is different. Our backgrounds, circumstances, and unique competencies are all different. Thus, our paths and stories are different. But despite all the differences, there is a common thread of qualities it takes to succeed: self-motivation, grit, curiosity, and persistence. It doesn't matter where you start, or where you currently are on your journey to becoming a Data Ninja, one thing remains true: **if you work hard, you will succeed.**

"Being the richest man in the cemetery doesn't matter to me. Going to bed at night saying we've done something wonderful, that's what matters to me."
~ *Steve Jobs*

It's Worth It

I hope the stories shared above have inspired you and provided some lessons. None of these individuals will tell you it was easy, but they'd definitely tell you **it was worth it**. They started off without much experience, but were able to get into the field and achieve their dreams. They studied a lot, and a lot of the studying they did was self-assigned. The start of my own journey was much like theirs.

If you have the ability to pay for and take formal training to boost your skills in some concepts, by all means, do that. If you don't have the means to get formal training, don't give up. You still have a way. Just look at me, a constant learner. I'm always attending conferences, buying books, subscribing to new podcasts, and scouring YouTube for instructional videos. Sometimes, I watch longer YouTube videos at 2x the speed in order to consume content quicker, and I use the **Threelly SmartView Extension** (www.threelly.com) to save specific time slices for further reference. At the end of the day, you have to optimize your time and tools to become an information consumption machine.

Self-education and the abundant availability of information on the internet today makes it easier than ever for *anyone* to master new concepts on your own and change your lives. Furthermore, as you learn new concepts, you'll eventually need a way to keep track of everything. For this, I use Google Drive heavily and keep a running folder in my Google Drive account of the concepts I learned or need to learn.

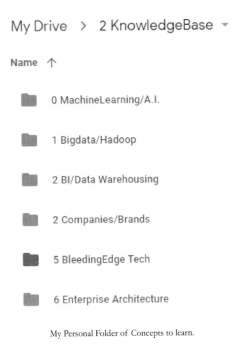

My Drive > 2 KnowledgeBase

Name ↑

📁 0 MachineLearning/A.I.

📁 1 Bigdata/Hadoop

📁 2 BI/Data Warehousing

📁 2 Companies/Brands

📁 5 BleedingEdge Tech

📁 6 Enterprise Architecture

My Personal Folder of Concepts to learn.

The image above is a list of just the few things on my radar. Yours could be different. Each folder of mine has different notes, content, and organization. As I learn these concepts, I keep the reference notes and links. That way, when a certain topic comes up in the future, I know where to look. This is the system that works for me, and I've used it for years with great success. But of course, you should find something that works for you. Use a personal wiki, a note app on your phone, *something*—it doesn't matter. As long as it is coherent and simple to you, that's all that counts.

Not Technical Enough?

One of the feedbacks I received during the review process of writing this book was that it's not technical enough—that it's just a reference book. I want to address that here.

I'm unapologetic about making this a reference book and not a technical book per se. I could explain all the concepts here for you to understand instead of providing reference materials for you to learn. In the beginning, I was tempted to do so, but quickly decided not to. Not only would that task be daunting, but it'd also be pointlessly redundant. As you can see, there are already tons of free and premium material on the internet that can teach you every single one of the concepts in this book and more. Why reinvent the wheel? People don't need more information, they need a game plan, and that's what I'm giving you.

"If you always do what you've always done, you'll always get what you've always got."
~Henry Ford

Even with a game plan in hand, you still have to execute in order to see results. Don't just read this book and run off. As writer, programmer, and avid student of life, Derek Sivers once said, **"If more information was the answer, then we'd all be billionaires with perfect abs."** Siver's statement couldn't get any truer or more brutally honest than that. We all know the lack of information isn't the problem. It's the *use* of that information—the execution—that counts.

You've got dreams to achieve, bills to pay, and a career in data analytics to realize. You've been provided with a solid game plan and lots of resources you can follow. The ball is now in your court. No more excuses! It's time to execute the play! What are you waiting for?

Words Of Inspiration

Congratulations! You've finished this book, have a game plan in place, and have decided to continue in the field of data analytics. Let me offer some advice and words of inspiration to make sure you continue on the right path and get the most enjoyment out of your newly-chosen career field.

As I mentioned in the beginning, this book is meant to be a game plan. And as in any sport or competitive game, not all the calls are made at once. You start with a few, and then make the calls as you progress through the game. My hope is you will have the necessary skills from this book to eventually take on the more foreign and sophisticated topics. And as the demand for things like data science, machine learning, IoT, and artificial intelligence continues to heat up, I will consider writing a companion book in those areas to help you continue your journey to becoming a well-rounded Data Analytics Ninja.

"A mind troubled by doubt cannot focus on the course to victory."
~Arthur Golden

As you read this book and study the concepts, remind yourself it might seem difficult at first. But as the saying goes, anything worth doing is difficult. Maybe you are the type of person who fears failure and is terrified to get started. Maybe this all sounds boring to you and you'd rather do something more interesting. Maybe this isn't the right time and you want to give yourself more time before you start. Whatever your reasons are, realize that those reasons are indeed EXCUSES and excuses usually sound more rational and convincing than you think. If they weren't, we'd all be actively working toward our goals and dreams.

This is meant to be a source of INSPIRATION. It's now up to you to take the resources, sharpen your Ninja skills, and bring it to the world. The world is waiting for you, so what are *you* waiting for?

Thank You

Thank you for giving me this opportunity to share some insights and resources with you through this book. Nothing pleases me more than helping people realize their professional and personal dreams while having meaningful impact in the world by analyzing data.

I look forward to hearing about how you've been able to put this book to work, and more importantly, hearing your stories of how you've leveraged your Ninja skills to help solve company problems and better your life.

If you work hard, take your time, build these skills and stay focused on the **Game Plan** presented in this book, you will succeed. You will indeed become a force to be reckoned with in the data analytics space, and thus, a true **Data Ninja**.

Acronyms

ACID	Atomicity, Consistency, Isolation and Durability
BI	Business Intelligence
CDA	Confirmatory Data Analysis
CRM	Customer Relationship Management
CSV	Comma-separated Values
DBA	Database Administrator
DCL	Data Control Language
DDL	Data Definition Language
DIKW	Data Information Knowledge Wisdom
DML	Data Modification Language
DWH	Data Warehouse
EDA	Exploratory Data Analysis
ERM	Entity Relationship Models
ETL	Extract Transform Load
HDFS	Hadoop Distributed File System
KPI	Key Performance Indicator
LOB	Line of Business
NoSQL	Not Only SQL
ODS	Operational Data Store
OLAP	Online Analytical Processes
OLTP	Online Transactional Processes
RDBMS	Relational Database Management System
SAS	Statistical Analysis Software
SQL	Structured Query Language
TCL	Transaction Control Language
XML	Extensible Markup Language

Glossary Of Definitions

Big Data
Big data is an evolving term that describes any voluminous amount of structured, semi-structured and unstructured data that has the potential to be mined for information. Although Big Data doesn't refer to any specific quantity, the term is often used when speaking about petabytes and exabytes of data.

Data Ninja
A Data Ninja is an entry level, unspecialized, entrepreneurial individual that works within a structured environment (usually within a company), employing a variety of tools and performing a variety of tasks related to collecting, organizing, and interpreting data to gain useful information.

Data Analysis
Data analysis is the process of finding the right data to answer a question, understanding how to mine a given dataset, discovering the important patterns in the data, and communicating your results to have the biggest possible impact.

Database
A database (abbreviated DB) is a collection of information that is organized so that it can easily be accessed, managed, and updated. A database basically helps to organize a collection of information in such a way that a computer program can quickly select desired pieces of data. Many datasets in companies are stored and manipulated in databases.

Data Warehousing
In computing, a data warehouse (DW or DWH), also known as an enterprise data warehouse (EDW), is a system used for reporting and data analysis. DWs are central repositories of integrated data from one or more disparate sources.

Dimensional Modeling

Dimensional modeling (DM) names a set of techniques and concepts used in data warehouse design. Many dimensional models typically consist of fact tables and lookup tables.

Predictive Analytics

Predictive analytics is the practice of extracting information from existing data sets in order to determine patterns and predict future possibilities and trends. It doesn't dictate the future, but it forecasts what might happen in the future with an acceptable level of reliability, and includes what-if scenarios and risk assessment.

Programming

Programming is the process of taking an algorithm and encoding it into a notation, a programming language, so that it can be executed by a computer. Programming involves activities such as analysis, developing understanding, generating algorithms, verification of requirements of algorithms (including their correctness and resource consumption), and implementation (commonly referred to as coding) of algorithms in a target programming language. Programming can be done in many different programming languages including C, FORTRAN, JavaScript, Lisp, Python, Ruby, and Smalltalk.

Figure Glossary

Figure 1: Data analysis tools used in the last 12 months (Nuggets)
Figure 2: Microsoft Excel screenshot (Excel)
Figure 3: The sky is literally the limit for using Microsoft Excel for dashboarding and presentation of data that tells a consistent and coherent story (Excel)
Figure 4: Data Warehouse ETL Architecture (serra)
Figure 5: Which programming tools to use for data analysis (kdnuggets)
Figure 6: Garter's Hype cycle (Gartner)
Figure 7: Revolutionary change cycle (hangthebankers.com)

Relevant Quotes Glossary

"We're entering a new world in which data may be more important than software." - Tim O'Reilly, Founder, O'Reilly Media

"The future belongs to those who believe in the beauty of their dreams." - Eleanor Roosevelt, Former First Lady of the United States

"Find out what you like doing best, and get someone to pay you for doing it." - Katharine Whitehorn, British Journalist

"No battle was ever won according to plan, but no battle was ever won without one." - Dwight D. Eisenhower, 34th President of the United States

"Numbers have an important story to tell. They rely on you to give them a clear and convincing voice." - Stephen Few, IT Expert and Author

"When the winds of change blow, some people build walls and others build windmills." - Chinese Proverb

"Only the wisest and stupidest of men never change." - Confucius, Chinese Philosopher

"Flexibility is a learned mental skill. In today's dynamic world, your effectiveness as a professional depends on your readiness to adjust quickly to the moments of need or opportunity, adversity, and change." - Jennifer Touma, Author

"What I try to focus on is not to try to stop the march of technological progress. Instead, I try to run faster." - Yuval Noah Harari, Author and Historian

"It is not the strongest of the species that survives, nor the most intelligent that survives. It is the one that is most adaptable to change." - Charles Darwin, Biologist

"Enjoying success requires the ability to adapt. Only by being open to change will you have a true opportunity to get the most from your talent." - Nolan Ryan, Major League Baseball Hall of Famer

"You are very powerful, provided you know how powerful you are." - Yogi Bhajan, Yoga Master

"Information technology and business are becoming inextricably interwoven. I don't think anybody can talk about one without talking about the other." - Bill Gates, Founder, Microsoft Inc.

"Stop being afraid of what could go wrong, and start being excited about what could go right." - Tony Robbins, Author and Entrepreneur

"Being the richest man in the cemetery doesn't matter to me. Going to bed at night saying we've done something wonderful, that's what matters to me." - Steve Jobs, Founder, Apple Inc.

"If you always do what you've always done, you'll always get what you've always got." - Henry Ford, Founder, Ford Motors

"A mind troubled by doubt cannot focus on the course to victory." - Arthur Golden, Author, Memoirs of a Geisha

Bibliography

(Information Governance Initiative), IGI. "http://iginitiative.com/biggest-risk-big-data-inability-extract-value/." 20 March 2015. "*IS THE BIGGEST RISK OF BIG DATA THE INABILITY TO EXTRACT VALUE?*". Article. 25 April 2015.

Bain. "http://www.bain.com/publications/articles/the-value-of-big-data. aspx." n.d. "*The Value of Big Data: How Analytics Differentiates Winners.*". Article. 24 March 2015.

Big Data Salary, "Inside Big Data Salary". *https://datajobs.com/big-data-salary.* n.d. Table. 25 March 2015.

Brown, Tim. "http://insights.som.yale.edu/insights/how-do-you-build-culture-innovation." n.d. "*How Do You Build a Culture of Innovation? - Yale Insights*". Article. 25 April 2015.

Carroll, Jim. "Chapter 7 - Creating an Innovation Culture." Carroll, Jim. "*What I Learned from Frogs in Texas: Saving Your Skin with Forward Thinking Innovation.*". Mississauga, Ont.: Oblio, 2004. 81. Print.

CDN. "http://cdn.images.express.co.uk/img/dynamic/78/590x/nelson-mandela-interprete-448108.jpg." 10 December 2013. *Figure 1: A sign language interpreter during a memorial service at FNB Stadium in honor of Nelson Mandela in Soweto, near Johannesburg.* Image. 20 April 2015.

coca-cola. "http://www.coca-colacompany.com/stories/program-or-perish-why-everyone-should-learn-to-code." n.d. "*Program or Perish: Why Everyone Should Learn to Code.*". report. 11 april 2015.

Cprogramming.com. "http://www.cprogramming.com/whyprogram.html." n.d. "*Why Learn to Program?*" . Article. 11 April 2015.

Datanami. "http://www.datanami.com/2014/10/02/top-three-things-excel/." 14 October 2014. *Top Three Things Not To Do in Excel.*". 11 April 2015.

Data-Warehouses. "http://data-warehouses.net/glossary/dimensionalmodel.html." n.d. *Dimensional Model.*". Diagram. 25 March 2015.

Dice. *Dice.com.* 20 April 2015. Search. 20 April 2015.

DNews. "http://news.discovery.com/tech/apps/youngest-video-game-programmer-130215.htm." n.d. *Meet the Youngest Video Game Programmer : DNews.*". Article. 11 April 2015.

Doyle, Martin. ""What Is the Difference Between Data and Information?"." n.d. *Business 2 Community.* Article. 25 March 2015.

EarSketch. "http://earsketch.gatech.edu/category/learning/anatomy-of-an-earsketch-project/what-is-programming." n.d. *"EarSketch.*" . quote. 11 April 2015.

Eridon, Corey. "http://blog.hubspot.com/marketing/problem-with-predictive-analytics." 11 June 2014. *The Problem With Predictive Analytics.* Article. 20 April 2015.

Eskimo. "https://www.eskimo.com/~scs/cclass/progintro/sx1.html." n.d. *"Skills Needed in Programming.*". Document. 11 april 2015.

Excel, Microsoft. *Pivot Functions within MS Excel.* 2015. Screenshot.

FastCompany. "http://www.fastcompany.com/most-innovative-companies/2014/industry/big-data." 10 February 2014. *"The World's Top 10 Most Innovative Companies in Big Data.*". Article. 24 April 2015.

Forbes. "http://www.forbes.com/sites/kashmirhill/2012/02/16/how-target-figured-out-a-teen-girl-was-pregnant-before-her-father-did/." n.d. *"How Target Figured Out A Teen Girl Was Pregnant Before Her Father Did.*".

Article. 19 April 2015.

Franks, Bill. "http://iianalytics.com/research/analytics-gone-wrong-dire-consequences-for-kids." 9 November 2011. "*Analytics Gone Wrong: Dire Consequences for Kids*". Article. 24 April 2015.

Gartner. "*Gartner Reveals Top Predictions for IT Organizations and Users for 2013 and Beyond*". 2013. Press Release. 25 March 2015.

—. "Gartner Says by 2016, 70 Percent of the Most Profitable Companies Will Manage Their Business Processes Using Real-Time Predictive Analytics or Extreme Collaboration." Analisys. 2015. Report.

gartner. *http://na2.www.gartner.com/imagesrv/newsroom/images/HC_ET_2014.jpg;pv4cc7877f7de80268*. 2014. chart. 2015.

GeekWire. "http://www.geekwire.com/2014/analysis-examining-computer-science-education-explosion/." n.d. "*Analysis: The Exploding Demand for Computer Science Education, and Why America Needs to Keep up*". Chart. 11 April 2015.

GeekWirre. "http://www.geekwire.com/2014/analysis-examining-computer-science-education-explosion/." n.d. "*Analysis: The Exploding Demand for Computer Science Education, and Why America Needs to Keep up* ". Chart. 11 April 2015.

Gigaom. " https://gigaom.com/2012/10/14/why-becoming-a-data-scientist-might-be-easier-than-you-think/." n.d. "*Why Becoming a Data Scientist Might Be Easier than You Think.*". quote. 11 april 2015.

—. "https://gigaom.com/2015/01/27/microsoft-throws-down-the-gauntlet-in-business-intelligence/." 2015. "*Microsoft Throws down the Gauntlet in Business Intelligence.*". 11 April 5015.

GlassDoor. *www.glassdoor.com*. 20 April 2015. Search. 20 April 2015.

HowTo. "http://howtostartprogramming.com/getting-started/." n.d. "*How To Start Programming.*". Document. 11 april 2015.

HTB. *http://www.hangthebankers.com/wp-content/uploads/2012/10/Stages-of-change.jpg*. 2015.

IBM. *http://www-03.ibm.com/press/us/en/pressrelease/27357.wss. 25 March 2015*. Article. 20 April 2015.

Illinois. "http://ori.hhs.gov/education/products/n_illinois_u/datamanagement/datopic.html." n.d. *"Data Analysis." Responsible Conduct of Research (RCR)*. Goverment Resource. 25 March 2015.

InformationBuilders. "http://www.informationbuilders.com/data-warehousing." n.d. *"Data Warehousing (Data Warehouse) Solutions | Information Builders*.". Article. 11 April 2015.

Jain, Piyanka. ""5 Steps To Transition Your Career To Analytics: Step 1 - Identify Your Ideal Job."." *Forbes Magazine* (2015, Jan 5). Article.

kdnuggets. "http://www.kdnuggets.com/2012/08/poll-analytics-data-mining-programming-languages.html." n.d. *"Poll Results: Top Languages for Analytics/data Mining Programming*.". poll. 11 april 2015.

Kearney, A. T. *"Big Data and the Creative Destructive of Today's Business Models*.". n.d. Table. 26 March 2015.

Kimbal. "http://www.kimballgroup.com/1997/08/a-dimensional-modeling-manifesto/." 2 August 1997. *"A Dimensional Modeling Manifesto - Kimball Group*.". Article. 11 April 2015.

Kristal, Murat. ""Mining Mountains of Data is Key for Canadian Businesses"." 12 September 2012. *The Globe and Mail*. Article. 25 March 2015. <http://www.theglobeandmail.com/report-on-business/cconomy/canada-competes/mining-mountains-of-data-is-key-for-canadian-businesses/article4540604/>.

Learn. "http://www.learn.geekinterview.com/database/sql/sql-standardization.html." 2015. *"SQL Standardization | Online Learning*.". Website. 20 April 2015.

Leek, Jeff. PhD. "https://www.coursera.org/course/dataanalysis." 2013. *Johns Hopkins Bloomberg School of Public Health: Data Analysis. Coursera Course.* Webpage. 25 March 2015.

Lifehacker. "http://lifehacker.com/5401954/programmer-101-teach-yourself-how-to-code." n.d. *"Programmer 101: Teach Yourself How to Code.".* instructions. 11 april 2015.

Longlivetheux. *DIKW Pyramid, Wikipedia.* 5 January 2015. DIKW Pyramid. 25 March 2015.

Marr, Bernard. "Big Data: Using Smart Big Data, Analytics and Metrics to Make Better Decisions and Improve Performance." Marr, Bernard. *Big Data: Using Smart Big Data, Analytics and Metrics to Make Better Decisions and Improve Performance.* n.d., 2015. Print.

McGee, Marianne Kolbasuk. "http://www.databreachtoday.com/prison-time-for-health-data-theft-a-5442." 23 January 2013. *"Prison Time for Health Data Theft."* Data Breach Today. Article. 25 March 2015.

McKinsey. "Big data: The Next Frontier for Innovation, Competition, and Productivity." Business Technology. 2011. Report.

ModelViewCulture. "https://modelviewculture.com/pieces/manufacturing-the-talent-shortage." n.d. *"Manufacturing the Talent Shortage.".* Document. 11 aprill 2015.

nde. "Data Warehouse ETL architecture." n.d. Chart.

NetworkWorld. "http://www.networkworld.com/article/2226514/tech-debates/what-s-better-for-your-big-data-application--sql-or-nosql-.html." n.d. *"What's Better for Your Big Data Application, SQL or NoSQL?".* 11 April 2015.

NewYorker. "http://www.newyorker.com/tech/elements/do-we-really-need-to-learn-to-code." n.d. *"Do We Really Need to Learn to Code?"* . quote. 11 april 2015.

Norvig. *http://norvig.com/21-days.html*. 2015. 2015.

Nuggets, K. D. "http://www.kdnuggets.com/polls/2011/tools-analytics-data-mining.html." May 2011. *"Data Mining/Analytic Tools Used."*. Poll. 11 April 2015.

Office, MS. "https://support.office.com/en-us/article/Use-the-Analysis-ToolPak-to-perform-complex-data-analysis-f77cbd44-fdce-4c4e-872b-898f4c90c007." n.d. *"Use the Analysis ToolPak to Perform Complex Data Analysis."*. Support. 11 April 2015.

Oracle. *"Big Data and the Creative Destructive of Today's Business Models"*. 2012. Chart. 25 March 2015.

Robert Half Technology, 2015 Salary Guide. *www.RHT.com*. 2015. Table. 25 March 2015.

Scott and Scott, technology Attorneys. "http://www.scottandscottllp.com/main/business_impact_of_data_breach.aspx." n.d. *"The Business Impact of Data Breach."*. Article. 26 March 2015.

Serra, James. *http://www.jamesserra.com/wp-content/uploads/2013/05/DataWarehouseWithMDMDQS2.jpg*. 2013. 2015.

Somerville, Richard. Interview. American climate scientist. 2011. Quote.

Stadd, Allison. ""Data Analysts: What you'll make and where you'll make it." 26 Movember 2014. *http://blog.udacity.com/2014/11/data-analysts-what-youll-make.html*. Web Article. 25 March 2015.

study.com. "http://study.com/become_a_data_analyst.html." 2015. *"Become a Data Analyst: Education and Career Roadmap."*. Chart. 26 March 2015.

Subramanyan, Vignesh. "http://www.business2community.com/business-intelligence/predictive-analytics-important-0610132." 9 September 2013.

"*Why Is Predictive Analytics Important?*" Business 2 Community. Article. 15 April 2015.

TechnologyCrowds. *www.TechnologyCrowds.com*. n.d. chart. 26 march 2015.

U.S. Census Bureau, Income and Poverty in the United States. *U.S. Department of Commerce Economics and Statistics Administration*. 2013. Census. 27 March 2015.

WFM. "https%3A%2F%2Fcareer4.successfactors. com%2Fcareer%3Fcareer_ns%3Djob_listing%26company%3DEA%26na vBarLevel%3DJOB_SEARCH%26rcm_site_locale%3Den_US%26career_ job_req_id%3D45383%26jobPipeline%3DIndeed." n.d. "*Career Opportunities: Data Analyst*". 24 March 2015.

Workable. ""Data Analyst Job Description. Ready to Post and Easy to Customize."." n.d. *http://resources.workable.com/data-analyst-job-description*. Job Description Resources. 26 March 2015.

Yale. "http%3A%2F%2Fits.yale.edu%2Fsecure-computing%2Fprotecting-yales-data%2Fsecure-removal-data-or-disposal-computing-devices." n.d. "*Secure Removal of Data or Disposal of Computing Devices*.". Article. 24 April 2015.

About The Author

Fru Nde is a technology professional who is very passionate about the Return on Investment (ROI) that companies can realize by effectively using their data assets. As a practicing Data Ninja, Fru uses his Ninja skills to help companies make sense of data, be it moving, storing, or analyzing data.

With over 12 years of experience in the tech field, Fru is a battle-tested speaker, trainer, mentor, coach, and consultant who has worked with corporations across the globe. Learn more about Fru at **www.frulouis.com**

 @FruLouis

 www.linkedin.com/in/frulouis

 www.frulouis.com

Made in the USA
Columbia, SC
11 April 2019